Level
4

Read and Succeed:
Comprehension

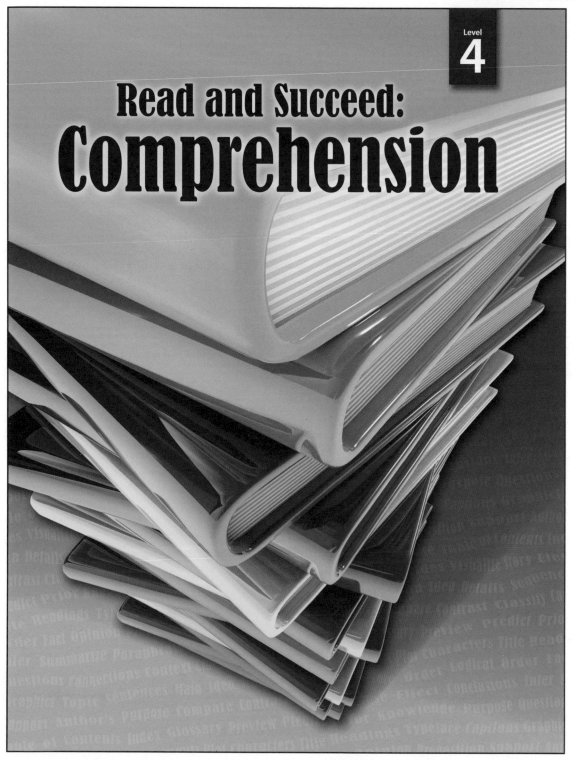

Consultant

Debra J. Housel, M.S.Ed.

SHELL EDUCATION

Contributing Authors

Timothy J. Bradley

Lisa Greathouse

Stephanie Paris

Greg Timmons

Publishing Credits

Dona Herweck Rice, *Editor-in-Chief*; Lee Aucoin, *Creative Director*; Don Tran, *Print Production Manager*; Timothy J. Bradley, *Illustration Manager*; Conni Medina, M.A.Ed., *Editorial Director*; Kristy Stark, M.A.Ed., *Editor*; Stephanie Reid, *Cover Designer*; Robin Erickson, *Interior Layout Designer*; Corinne Burton, M.S.Ed., *Publisher*

Shell Education

5301 Oceanus Drive
Huntington Beach, CA 92649-1030
http://www.shelleducation.com

ISBN 978-1-4258-0727-6

©2010 Shell Educational Publishing, Inc.

Table of Contents

Introduction

Comprehension is the goal of every reading task. The *Read and Succeed: Comprehension* series can help lay the foundation of comprehension skills that are essential for a lifetime of learning. The series was written specifically to provide the purposeful practice students need in order to succeed in reading comprehension. The more students practice, the more confident and capable they can become.

Why You Need This Book

- **It is standards based**. The skill practice pages are aligned to the Mid-continent Research for Education and Learning (McREL) standards. (See page 7.)
- **It has focused lessons**. Each practice page covers a key comprehension skill. Skills are addressed multiple times to provide several opportunities for mastery.
- **It employs advanced organization**. Having students encounter the question page first gives them a "heads up" when they approach the text, thereby enhancing comprehension and promoting critical-thinking abilities.
- **It has appropriate reading levels**. All passages have a grade level calculated based on the Shell Education leveling system, which was developed under the guidance of Dr. Timothy Rasinski, along with the staff at Shell Education.
- **It has an interactive whiteboard-compatible Teacher Resource CD.** This can be used to enhance instruction and support literacy skills.

How to Use This Book

First, determine what sequence will best benefit your students. Work through the book in order (as the skills become progressively more difficult) to cover all key skills. For reinforcement of specific skills, select skills as needed.

Then determine what instructional setting you will use. See below for suggestions for a variety of instructional settings:

Whole-Class or Small-Group Instruction	Independent Practice or Centers	Homework
Read and discuss the Skill Focus. Write the name of the skill on the board.	Create a folder for each student. Include a copy of the selected skill practice page and passage.	Give each student a copy of the selected skill practice page and passage.
Read and discuss responses to each question. Read the text when directed (as a group, in pairs, or individually).	Have students complete the skill practice page. Remind them to begin by reading the Skill Focus and to read the passage when directed.	Have students complete the skill practice page. Remind them to begin by reading the Skill Focus and to read the passage when directed.
Read and discuss the Critical Thinking question. Allow time for discussion before having students write their responses.	Collect the skill practice pages and check students' answers. Or, provide each student with a copy of the answer key (pages 138–149).	Collect the skill practice pages and check students' answers. Or, provide each student with a copy of the answer key (pages 138–149).

Research Support for the
Read and Succeed: Comprehension Series

Comprehension is the ability to derive meaning from text. It is critically important not only for the development of children's reading skills but also for students' abilities to obtain a complete education. The National Reading Panel (2000) states that comprehension is an active process that requires an intentional interaction between the reader and the text. A reader must engage in problem-solving thinking processes in order to relate the ideas represented in print to his or her own knowledge and experiences and build mental images to store in memory.

Teaching students to use specific strategies can improve their comprehension. To some degree, readers acquire such strategies informally. However, the National Reading Panel confirmed that explicit instruction in comprehension strategies is highly effective in enhancing understanding. That's why the *Read and Succeed: Comprehension* series was created: to make teaching comprehension strategies simple and time efficient. This book teaches specific strategies students can use to help them understand what they are reading.

Having students know in advance the questions they will be asked helps them to attend to the material. It gives them a focus as they read. It helps them to look for clues and to identify information they will need to remember. But most importantly, it allows them to organize information in their minds, building neural pathways that will be used again and again. Essentially, having a focus as they read teaches children how to think. This is why the skill practice page always appears before the reading passage in *Read and Succeed: Comprehension.*

Teaching a combination of reading comprehension techniques is the most effective approach for instruction. When students use strategies appropriately, they can improve their recall, question answering, question generation, and summarization of texts. Also, used in combination, these techniques can improve results in standardized comprehension tests. Yet teaching reading comprehension strategies to students at all grade levels can be complex. The *Read and Succeed: Comprehension* series was designed to make this process straightforward. Each book contains 65 lessons. Each lesson has a specific focus to concentrate on an important reading skill for a fiction or a nonfiction text. Step by step, students will learn the grade-level-appropriate skills they need to read and understand a wide variety of texts.

Each skill activity is independent; they need not be done in a certain order. However, it is in students' best interest to complete all of the activities. Using the *Read and Succeed: Comprehension* series will save you time and effort while simultaneously providing students with the vital skills needed to achieve 21st century comprehension and critical-thinking skills.

National Institute of Child Health and Human Development. 2000. *Report of the National Reading Panel. Teaching children to read: An evidence-based assessment of the scientific research literature on reading and its implications for reading instruction* (NIH Publication No. 00-4769). Washington, DC: U.S. Government Printing Office.

Standards Correlations

Shell Education is committed to producing educational materials that are research and standards based. In this effort, we have correlated all of our products to the academic standards of all 50 states, the District of Columbia, and the Department of Defense Dependent Schools.

How to Find Standards Correlations

To print a customized correlation report of this product for your state, visit our website at **www.shelleducation.com** and follow the on-screen directions. If you require assistance in printing correlation reports, please contact Customer Service at 1-877-777-3450.

Purpose and Intent of Standards

The No Child Left Behind legislation mandates that all states adopt academic standards that identify the skills students will learn in kindergarten through grade twelve. While many states had already adopted academic standards prior to NCLB, the legislation set requirements to ensure the standards were detailed and comprehensive.

Standards are designed to focus instruction and guide adoption of curricula. Standards are statements that describe the criteria necessary for students to meet specific academic goals. They define the knowledge, skills, and content students should acquire at each level. Standards are also used to develop standardized tests to evaluate students' academic progress.

Teachers are required to demonstrate how their lessons meet state standards. State standards are used in development of all of our products, so educators can be assured they meet the academic requirements of each state.

McREL Compendium

We use the Mid-continent Research for Education and Learning (McREL) Compendium to create standards correlations. Each year, McREL analyzes state standards and revises the compendium. By following this procedure, McREL is able to produce a general compilation of national standards. Each lesson in this product is based on one or more McREL standards. The chart on the following page lists each standard taught in this product and the page numbers for the corresponding lessons.

McREL Correlations Chart

Skill	Skill Focus and Page Numbers
Previews text	*Preview*, 8–9, 10–11
Establishes a purpose for reading	*Set a Purpose*, 20–21, 22–23; *Ask Questions*, 24–25, 26–27
Makes, confirms, and revises predictions	*Predict*, 12–13, 14–15; *Visualize*, 36–37, 38–39
Uses a variety of context clues to decode unknown words	*Context Clues*, 32–33, 34–35
Uses word reference materials (e.g., glossary) to determine the meaning, pronunciation, and derivations of unknown words	*Glossary*, 134–135, 136–137
Understands author's purpose or point of view	*Author's Purpose*, 94–95, 96–97
Uses reading skills and strategies to understand and interpret a variety of literary texts	*Story Elements*, 40–41, 42–43
Understands the basic concept of plot	*Plot*, 44–45, 46–47
Understands elements of character development	*Characters*, 48–49, 50–51
Makes connections between characters or events in a literary work and people or events in his or her own life	*Make Connections*, 28–29, 30–31
Uses reading skills and strategies to understand and interpret a variety of informational texts	*Fact and Opinion*, 86–87, 88–89; *Classify*, 102–103, 104–105; *Draw Conclusions*, 110–111, 112–113; *Infer*, 114–115, 116–117
Uses text organizers (e.g., headings, topic and summary sentences, graphic features, typeface, chapter titles) to determine the main ideas and to locate information in a text	*Title and Headings*, 52–53, 54–55; *Typeface and Captions*, 56–57, 58–59; *Graphics*, 60–61, 62–63; *Topic Sentences*, 64–65, 66–67
Identifies the main idea and supporting details	*Main Idea*, 68–69, 70–71; *Details*, 72–73, 74–75; *Main Idea and Details*, 76–77
Uses the various parts of a book to locate information (e.g., table of contents, index)	*Table of Contents*, 126–127, 128–129; *Index*, 130–131, 132–133
Summarizes and paraphrases information in texts	*Summarize*, 118–119, 120–121; *Paraphrase*, 122–123, 124–125
Uses prior knowledge and experience to understand and respond to new information	*Prior Knowledge*, 16–17, 18–19
Understands structural patterns or organization in informational texts (e.g., chronological, logical, or sequential order; compare and contrast; cause and effect; proposition and support)	*Chronological Order*, 78–79, 80–81; *Logical Order*, 82–83, 84–85; *Proposition and Support*, 90–91, 92–93; *Compare and Contrast*, 98–99, 100–101; *Cause and Effect*, 106–107, 108–109

Preview

Looking at the title, pictures, and headings before you read helps you to get ready to understand the text.

1. Preview the text. What do you already know about recipes?

    _____

    _____

    _____

2. How is the text similar to other recipes you may have seen?

    _____

    _____

3. Read the recipe. Is there anything about this recipe that surprises you?

    _____

    _____

Critical Thinking

Why is it wise to preview a recipe before you start to make the item?

_____

_____

_____

Apricot Banana Shake

Ingredients You Will Need:

- 1 cup orange juice, chilled
- $\frac{1}{2}$ cup milk
- $\frac{1}{4}$ teaspoon vanilla
- 1 16-ounce can pitted apricot halves, chilled
- 1 banana
- ground nutmeg

Equipment You Will Need:

- measuring cups
- can opener
- blender
- drinking glasses

Directions:

1. Measure the orange juice, milk, and vanilla into the blender. Add the apricots and their juice. Peel the banana. Break the banana into four pieces; add to the blender container.

2. With help from an adult, put the lid on the blender and blend the mixture until it is smooth. Pour the mixture into the glasses; sprinkle the top with a little nutmeg.

Serve cold and enjoy.

Makes four servings.

Preview

Skill Focus

Looking at the title, pictures, and headings before you read helps you to get ready to understand the text.

1. Scan the headings. Will this text be about famous skateboarders, skateboarding tricks, or how skateboards have changed over time?

   _____

2. Look for dates below the headings. Write each date on a line below.

   _____

   _____

   _____

   _____

   _____

3. Read the text. Then, next to each date above, write what happened in the history of skateboarding.

Critical Thinking

How did previewing help you to understand the text when you read it?

_____

_____

_____

The Origins of Skateboarding

The sport of skateboarding has had more ups and downs than a skate park.

In the Beginning

The earliest form of the skateboard dates back to the early 1900s. It was nothing more than a scooter made with roller skates, a two-by-four piece of lumber, and a wooden crate. Another piece of wood at the top of the crate served as the handles.

1950s Version

It wasn't until the 1950s that the crate and handles were removed. Kids started riding hands free. That's when skateboarding was truly born. Every kid wanted a skateboard! By 1959, skateboards hit store shelves. A few years later, professional skateboarders were wowing crowds.

The Safety Issue

Those first boards were dangerous, though. Steel wheels felt choppy. Clay wheels were unsafe. After serious injuries were reported, the popularity of skateboarding went downhill. Stores stopped selling them. Cities banned them. By 1965, the sport was almost dead.

Better Wheels

In 1975, new skateboards were made with better wheels. They were made of urethane, a type of rubber. The ride was smoother and safer. New skateboards designs had a kick tail that turned up at the end. The new design made tricks possible. Skateboards were hot again!

Ups and Downs

Since then, skateboarding has gone up and down in popularity. Today, skateboarding video games help to fuel its popularity. Many cities have built concrete skate parks with ramps and rails for tricks. Competitions are held around the world. Some enthusiasts even want to make skateboarding an Olympic sport.

Predict

Look for clues to help you guess what is coming next in the text.

1. Look at the title and picture. What do you think this story will be about?

    _____

    _____

2. In this story, Black Beauty's mother gives him advice. What do you think she will say to him?

    _____

3. Read the story. What does Black Beauty's mother want him to be?

    _____

4. Reread the last paragraph. What do you predict about Black Beauty's actions in the future?

    _____

    _____

Critical Thinking

How did your predictions for questions 1–2 compare with what actually happened in the story?

_____

_____

_____

Black Beauty

by Anna Sewell

Excerpt from Chapter 1: *My Early Home*

There were six young colts in the meadow besides me. They were older than I was; some were nearly as large as grown-up horses. I used to run with them and had great fun. We used to gallop all together round and round the field as hard as we could go. Sometimes we had rather rough play, for they would frequently bite and kick as well as gallop.

One day, when there was a good deal of kicking, my mother whinnied to me to come to her. She told me, "I wish you to pay attention to what I am going to say to you. The colts who live here are very good colts, but they are cart-horse colts. Of course, they have not learned manners. You have been well-bred and well-born. Your father has a great name in these parts, and your grandfather won the cup two years at the Newmarket races. Your grandmother had the sweetest temper of any horse I ever knew, and you have never seen me kick or bite. I hope you will grow up gentle and good, and never learn bad ways. Do your work with a good will, lift your feet up well when you trot, and *never* bite or kick, even in play."

I have never forgotten my mother's advice. I knew she was a wise horse, and our master thought a great deal of her. Her name was Duchess, but he called her "Pet."

Predict

Look for clues to help you guess what is coming next in the text.

1. Read each sentence in the first column of the chart below. In the second column, make a prediction as to what will happen next.

Sentence	Your Prediction	What Actually Happened
Emily chased the rabbit into the woods behind the wagons, but it disappeared.		
Emily tried another direction, but soon found that that was wrong, too.		
Emily sank to the ground and started to cry.		

2. Read the story. Then fill in the third column of the chart above.

Critical Thinking

How did making predictions help you to understand what you read?

_____

_____

_____

Emily in Trouble

The wagon train had been traveling for weeks now, and Emily was getting bored and tired—tired of not having a real bed to sleep in or a real home. She was bored because there was never anything fun for a girl her age to do. Mama promised it wouldn't be too much longer, but the trip seemed to take forever.

Then, one day, a rabbit caught Emily's eye. Maybe she could catch it, and then she'd have a pet! Emily chased the rabbit into the woods behind the wagons, but it disappeared. Emily looked and looked for it, but at last she gave up. She turned to go back, but nothing looked familiar. She started in one direction, but it was the wrong way. Emily tried another direction, but soon found that that was wrong, too.

Emily was frightened. What if she couldn't find the wagons? What if they didn't realize she was missing and just kept moving farther and farther away from her? What if some vicious wild animal attacked her?

Emily sank to the ground and started to cry . . . but wait . . . did she hear voices? She stood up and ran toward them. As she got closer, she recognized Mama's voice and the voices of some of the men from the train. Then she could see them. Emily ran as fast as she could, right into Mama's welcoming arms.

Mama carried Emily back to their wagon and put her to bed. Emily was glad she was home. Home was wherever Mama was. She'd never complain about being bored again.

Prior Knowledge

Whenever you read, you bring what you already know about the subject to the text. You use this prior knowledge to make sense of the new information you read.

1. Read the title. Write two things that you already know about crayons.

   _____

   _____

2. Read the text. Draw a picture to show how a crayon mold might look.

   ┌───┐
   │   │
   │   │
   │   │
   │   │
   │   │
   └───┘

3. Did the two favorite crayon colors surprise you? Explain.

   _____

   _____

Critical Thinking

How would reading this text be more difficult if you had never used a crayon?

_____

_____

_____

Making Crayons

Did you know that blue and red are the most well-liked crayon colors? Next to coffee and peanut butter, a crayon's smell is the most recognizable smell there is. If you're like the average kid, by the time you are 10 years old, you will have used about 730 crayons!

Crayons are made out of two things—pigment and wax. *Pigment* means color. More than 120 colors can be made. The wax is the same kind that's used in candles. First, the pigment and wax are heated. After the mixture melts, it's poured into molds. The molds have many crayon-shaped holes. Next, the molds are dunked in cold water to harden the wax. They take less than 10 minutes to cool. A single mold can make 1,200 crayons at a time!

When cooled, the crayons are pushed out of the mold and checked by workers. Crayons that are not perfect or have broken tips get melted again. Before the 1940s, each crayon was hand wrapped. Now they're wrapped by machines and then boxed.

So, the next time you get out your box of crayons, think about what went into making them.

Prior Knowledge

Whenever you read, you bring what you already know about the subject to the text. You use this prior knowledge to make sense of the new information you read.

1. Write one thing that you already know about fundraising.

   _____

   _____

2. Write one thing you already know about recycling.

   _____

   _____

3. Read the text. How did Jen find a way to use recycling to raise money?

   _____

   _____

   _____

Critical Thinking

How did thinking about what you already knew about fundraising and recycling help you to understand this text?

   _____

   _____

   _____

Trash to Treasure

Jen didn't know how her school dance team would be able to afford to travel to Florida for the national competition. It was tough enough just to raise money for costumes. What were they going to do? As team captain, Jen felt she needed to come up with an idea.

At lunch, Jen noticed how many students were throwing empty soda and water bottles in the trash. A recycling program had been started a few years back, but it had ended. Nobody had wanted to bring the bags of bottles to the recycling center.

Jen saw an opportunity. She went to see the principal. "If members of our team pick up the recyclable bottles every few days, may we use the money we collect at the recycling center for our dance team?" Jen asked.

"I think that's a great idea, Jen," Ms. Weaver said. "But if another club wants to take over next season, I'll have to give them a chance, too."

Jen agreed that that was fair. She ran to the dance team advisor to give her the good news.

Jen knew that the money raised from empty water bottles might not be enough to get them all the way to Florida. But they were a lot closer now than they were before.

Set a Purpose

Before you read, ask yourself a question about the text based on the pictures or the title. Then read to find the answer. Having a purpose will help you to get more out of what you read.

1. Look at the title and picture. Write a question that you hope the text will answer.

   _____

2. Read the text. Write two things you learned about dolphins.

   _____

   _____

3. Which of the text's paragraphs do you wish included more information? Explain.

   _____

   _____

Critical Thinking

Did the text answer your question? If not, how can you find the answer?

_____

_____

_____

Delightful Dolphins

Dolphins have always fascinated people. The ancient Greeks put pictures of them on coins and painted their images on walls. Sailors believed that dolphins swimming next to their ships meant good luck on the voyage.

Dolphins are not fish; in fact, they eat fish. They are sea mammals. Fish have fins, while dolphins have flippers. When fish swim, they move their tails from side to side. When dolphins swim, they move their tails up and down. Fish breathe in water, but dolphins have to rise to the water's surface occasionally to take a breath.

Dolphins use sounds to find things. They send out clicking sounds, and the sounds strike an object and bounce back to the dolphins. They use the sounds to tell where the object is located. They also use these sounds to communicate with one another.

If you go to an aquarium or a zoo, you may see bottle-nosed dolphins. They look like they are always smiling. They are so intelligent that they can learn how to do tricks, such as throwing balls through nets and jumping through hoops. They can even be trained to "walk" on the water using their strong tails.

Dolphins seem to be interested in humans. There have been numerous reports of dolphins coming to the rescue of swimmers who were drowning or being attacked by a shark. In 2007, a great white shark bit a surfer twice. Then a pod of dolphins surrounded the injured man, keeping the shark away so he could reach the shore.

Set a Purpose

Before you read, ask yourself a question about the text based on the pictures or the title. Then read to find the answer. Having a purpose will help you to get more out of what you read.

1. Look at the title and picture. Write a question that you hope the text will answer.

   _____

2. What will this text be about? How do you know?

   _____

   _____

3. Read the text. Write two things you learned about how companies encourage you to buy their products in the grocery store.

   _____

   _____

Critical Thinking

Did the text answer your question? If not, how can you find the answer?

_____

_____

_____

Be a Careful Shopper

When you go to the grocery store, have you ever thought about why you choose certain things and not others? Sure, you may have a shopping list. But there are lots of ads and promotions trying to get you to buy things that aren't on that list.

Companies try to make their food seem really tasty in TV commercials. Sometimes they use a song or phrase they hope you'll remember when you get to the store. There are people who get paid to decide where products are placed in the store. They might set up a special display near the entrance. They want you to notice the display as soon as you walk in.

Companies pay to have their products placed on the shelves right at eye level so you'll be sure to see them as you walk down the aisle. And then, there are those people who offer you goodies on little plates as you walk by. The idea is that once you taste the food, you will buy it.

Think carefully the next time you go shopping. Are you buying just what you need? Or are you buying things just because someone is trying to sell them to you?

Ask Questions

Before you read, ask yourself, "What questions do I have about this topic? What do I hope to learn?" Then, as you read, look for the answers.

1. Look at the title and picture. What do you think this story will be about?

   _____

2. What do you think the inflatable gorilla has to do with the story?

   _____

3. Read the text. Write two facts from the text. (Remember, facts can be proven true.)

   _____

   _____

4. If you were the reporter and wanted to know more of the story, what question would you ask and why?

   _____

Critical Thinking

Did you like how this text was written in a question-and-answer format? Explain why or why not.

_____

_____

_____

THE GORILLA CAPER

Reporter: So, Chief Jenkins, can you explain what happened out here last night?

Chief Jenkins: Sure, Ken. It seems that some people thought it would be funny to steal the giant inflatable gorilla from the top of a car dealership. We're not sure how they got it down without anyone seeing them.

Reporter: Have you found it?

Chief Jenkins: Yes. It turned up this morning.

Reporter: Where?

Chief Jenkins: We got a call from the principal at Maple Hills High School. The gorilla was on the football field this morning.

Reporter: Any idea who took it?

Chief Jenkins: We're still not sure. Since Maple Hills is playing Lincoln High in the big game tonight, we're guessing it's a Lincoln High prank.

Reporter: Is the gorilla back at the dealership?

Chief Jenkins: No. The dealership's owner thought the gorilla should stay at Maple Hills until the game is over.

Reporter: Why is that?

Chief Jenkins: Well, he graduated from Maple Hills. And he said that the gorilla always brings him good luck!

Ask Questions

Before you read, ask yourself, "What questions do I have about this topic? What do I hope to learn?" Then, as you read, look for the answers.

1. Look at the title. Write two things that you already know about this topic in the first column of the chart below.

What I Know	What I Want to Know	What I Learned

2. What do you want to know about this topic? Write two questions that you hope the text will answer in the second column of the chart.

3. Read the text. Write the answers to your questions in the third column.

Critical Thinking

If one of your questions was not answered, how can you find the answer?

_____

_____

_____

Will the Real Tasmanian Devil Please Stand Up?

Have you ever heard of a Tasmanian devil? Does the name make you think of a cartoon character? Did you know that there really is a Tasmanian devil? It comes from Tasmania, which is an island off the coast of Australia.

The Tasmanian devil is an animal about the size of a large dog. It can grow to be about 30 inches (0.8 m) long. It can weigh up to 22 pounds (10 kg). A female is smaller than a male. Some people say a Tasmanian devil looks like a bear cub. It has dark fur. Its jaws are large. Its teeth are strong.

Its name comes from the devilish look on its face. It has a hoarse snarl and a bad temper, too. You might think it would be a good hunter, but the Tasmanian devil is actually lazy. Rather than hunt for its own food, it lets others hunt. It eats the leftovers from other predators' kills. It will eat bones, fur, and everything else.

Tasmanian devils sleep during the day. They're nocturnal, or awake at night. They're easy to hear at night because they are such noisy eaters.

At one time, Tasmanian devils almost became extinct. They were killed off by dingoes, which are wild dogs in Australia. Tasmanian devils are now a protected species, so their numbers are increasing again.

Make Connections

When you read, try to think of a situation in your own life that is similar. This is called making connections.

1. Briefly tell about a time when your family chose to do something you didn't look forward to doing.

   _____

   _____

2. Read the story. Tell about a time when you were glad to meet someone.

   _____

   _____

3. Whose personality is more like yours—Abby or Luke? Explain.

   _____

4. Would you like to vacation on a cruise ship? Explain.

   _____

Critical Thinking

How did making connections to your own life help you to enjoy this story?

_____

_____

_____

Bon Voyage

"Bon voyage!" the taxi driver said as Abby and her family got out of the cab, unloaded their suitcases, and headed toward the ship.

"Why do people always say 'Bon voyage' when you're going on a trip?" Abby grumbled.

"It's French for 'Have a good journey,'" Abby's mom said cheerfully.

Abby knew that, but she just felt like complaining. Abby was unhappy about her family's vacation. Sure, it was a cool cruise ship, but Abby really wanted to spend winter break at home with her friends instead of with her parents and younger brother. Even with all of the activities on the ship, Abby was convinced that the next six days would be b-o-r-i-n-g.

As soon as her family settled into their cramped cabin, Abby decided to go for a walk around the ship.

"I want to come!" her six-year-old brother, Luke, pleaded.

"It's starting already," Abby thought. She knew that her parents were going to tell her to take her brother. "Okay, you can come," Abby agreed glumly. "But you'd better not give me any trouble."

As soon as they opened the door, they saw a girl stepping out of the cabin next door. The girls looked at each other and smiled.

"Hi! I'm Luke. What's your name?" Without pausing for an answer, Luke continued his rapid-fire questioning. "You look about the same age as Abby. She's 11. How old are you? Where are you from? What grade are you in? Do you have any brothers or sisters?"

Luke finally took a breath, and the two girls looked at each other and erupted in laughter.

"Luke sure knows how to break the ice, huh?" Abby said. "We were just going to go for a walk. Want to join us?"

"Sure," the girl replied.

Abby smiled. Maybe this wouldn't be such a bad vacation after all.

Make Connections

When you read, try to think of a situation in your own life that is similar. This is called making connections.

1. Would you like to go camping? Explain.

   _____

   _____

2. Read the story. Why did David choose Evan to go with him instead of his best friend?

   _____

   _____

   _____

3. What could David have done if Evan hadn't given the speech?

   _____

   _____

Critical Thinking

What do you think about David's choice?

_____

_____

_____

Choosing a Camping Buddy

David loved camping with his family. They would load up their truck with a tent, portable stove, chairs, flashlights, and everything else they needed for a weekend at their favorite state park campsite. And then there was the food: hot dogs cooked over the fire, baked potatoes in foil, and toasted marshmallows for dessert.

This time, David was especially excited. His mom had told him that he could bring a friend. That would be so much cooler than hanging out with his younger sister! But whom should he ask? Jack was his best friend, but David couldn't really imagine Jack out in the woods. Jack was into video games and anything electronic. The next day at school, David's friend, Evan, had to give a speech about his favorite hobby in front of the class.

"There's nothing I love more than camping," Evan said. "I wish I could go every weekend."

"Well, that was easy!" David said to himself. Evan was an obvious choice.

Context Clues

If you come to a new word that you do not know, reread the sentence in which it is found. If that doesn't work, keep reading. Information after the word may give you a clue as to what it means.

1. Scan the text for the words in boldface. These are words that you may never have seen before. Write the three words below.

   _____   _____   _____

2. Read the text. What is an *igloo*? _____

   How do you know?   _____

3. What does the word *insulator* mean? _____

   How do you know?   _____

4. What does the word *construct* mean? _____

   How do you know? _____

Critical Thinking

How did reading the text help you to make a picture in your mind of the inside of an igloo?

_____

_____

_____

A CHILLY HOME

How would you like to live in a house made of ice? If you're an Inuit child, that's where you might sleep on winter nights.

If you live in some parts of Canada and Greenland, your father or grandfather might build your family an **igloo**. You would live there in winter while the adults in your family fish or hunt. An igloo is a temporary home made out of blocks of snow or ice. The snow acts as an **insulator**. It keeps the cold air out and keeps the warm air in.

To **construct** an igloo, a builder places a row of blocks in an open circle on the snow-covered ground. Each block is about 2 feet (0.6 m) wide by 4 feet (1.2 m) long. The blocks are cut in a special way. They must slant toward the middle of the circle. Cutting and stacking them in this way makes the layers form a dome shape. A large hole at the top allows air in and smoke out. A fire burns in the igloo's center to keep the family warm.

The builder fills any cracks or open spaces in the walls with snow and ice. Then a small tunnel is added as an entrance. To keep out the wind, an animal hide covers the doorway. Since the Inuit have been building igloos for hundreds of years, they know how to work fast. The whole project takes just a few hours!

Context Clues

If you come to a new word that you do not know, reread the sentence in which it is found. If that doesn't work, keep reading. Information after the word may give you a clue as to what it means.

1. Read the story. What is the meaning of the word *distressed*?

    _____

    What clues did you use? _____

2. What is the meaning of the word *eavesdrop*?

    _____

    What clues did you use? _____

3. What is the meaning of the word *dawned*?

    _____

    What clues did you use? _____

Critical Thinking

How does using context help you to understand more difficult texts?

_____

_____

_____

Lost Eddie

Katrina was getting ready for bed when she heard the doorbell ring.

"Who could that be at the door so late?" she wondered. Katrina heard her mom open the door and start talking to another woman. The voice sounded like it belonged to their next-door neighbor, Marsha Jackson. She sounded very **distressed**.

"Eddie's missing," Ms. Jackson told Katrina's mom. "We haven't seen him since this morning." Katrina didn't know who Eddie was. She quietly tiptoed down the stairs to **eavesdrop.**

"Did the Jacksons have a relative visiting?" Katrina wondered. "Who could Eddie be?"

Katrina heard her mom invite Ms. Jackson in for a cup of tea. The two women sat at the kitchen table, and Katrina had to strain to listen. Katrina's mom asked where Eddie was last seen.

"He was left out in the backyard," Ms. Jackson broke down and wept. "I think he may have dug a hole under the fence and escaped."

That's when it **dawned** on Katrina—the Jacksons had just adopted a dog from the animal shelter last week. When they brought him home, he ran up to Katrina and licked her face. She hadn't known that they had named him Eddie.

"At least he has a license on his collar," Katrina's mom said. "Hopefully, someone will find him and return him."

Finally, Katrina couldn't stand it anymore. She ran downstairs and gave Ms. Jackson a hug.

"I'll wake up early and put up 'Lost Dog' posters all over the neighborhood," Katrina said. "I'm sure we'll find him."

Visualize

When you visualize, you form mental images based on what you read. It is like making a movie in your mind.

1. Read the first paragraph. Draw the picture you made in your mind of Libya's flag.

2. Read the second paragraph. Draw the picture you made in your mind of the French flag.

3. Read the remaining text. Draw the picture you made in your mind of the Japanese flag.

Critical Thinking

How does making pictures in your mind help you to understand what you read?

_____

_____

_____

Flags of the World

Most of the world's countries have flags with at least two of eight colors. These colors are yellow, orange, red, black, white, brown, blue, and green. Libya's flag is unique because it is solid green.

Many flags have vertical stripes, such as the three stripes on the Italian flag—one green, one white, and one red. The French flag is similar, but its stripes are blue, white, and red. Other flags have horizontal stripes, such as the Russian flag. Its stripes are white, blue, and red from top to bottom. The three stripes of the German flag are also horizontal. From top to bottom they are black, red, and yellow.

Italian flag

Some flags have symbols. The flag of Japan is white with a large red circle in the center to represent the sun. Both the Congo and Chinese flags have stars. Stars and crescents appear together on many flags. The flag of Turkey has one star and one crescent.

Some flags have stripes and symbols. The flag of Canada has one white and two red vertical stripes. In the middle of the white stripe is a large red maple leaf. The flag of Lebanon has horizontal red, white, and red stripes. It has a large green cedar (pine) tree in the middle of the white stripe.

Russian flag

Think of your country's flag. What does it look like? Does it have stripes? Does it have symbols? Find out the meaning of the symbols and colors of your flag.

Visualize

When you visualize, you form mental images based on what you read. It is like making a movie in your mind.

1. Read the first paragraph. Draw the picture you formed in your mind.

2. Read the second paragraph. Draw the picture you formed in your mind.

3. Read the rest of the text. Draw the picture you formed in your mind.

Critical Thinking

How did picturing the story as it occurred help you to understand it?

_____

_____

_____

The Shepherd and the Wild Sheep

A Fable by Aesop

One evening, as a shepherd gathered his flock from the field, he found some wild sheep among them. He put the wild sheep in the stable with his own sheep.

The next day it snowed, so he could not take the herd out and kept them in the stable. He gave his own sheep very little food and fed the wild sheep more. He hoped that they would want to stay with him and thus enlarge his herd.

When the snow melted, the shepherd took all the sheep out. The wild sheep immediately ran away. The shepherd ran after them. He caught up to them at the base of the mountain. The shepherd scolded the sheep for leaving and reminded them that during the storm, he had taken better care of them than of his own sheep.

One sheep said, "That is why we won't stay. Since you treated us better than the sheep you have tended for so long, if others came after us, you would treat them better than us." Then the wild sheep turned and fled.

Moral: New friends should not be treated better than old friends.

Story Elements

Every story has three elements: characters, a setting, and a plot. The plot is the problem and the way it gets resolved.

1. Before you read the story, glance at each paragraph. There are three characters. What are their names?

   _____   _____   _____

2. Read the story. Describe this story's setting (where and when the story happens).

   _____

   _____

3. A story's plot has two parts. The first is a conflict (problem). The second is how the problem is solved. What is the conflict in this story?

   _____

4. How is the conflict solved?

   _____

   _____

Critical Thinking

Predict what will happen next in the story.

_____

_____

_____

Racing a Tornado

If the girls had known what was going to happen, they never would have gotten on their bikes. But in the morning, it looked like it would be a perfect day for a long bike ride. Maria and Ariel set out at 7 A.M. and didn't stop for lunch until noon. They sat under an oak tree and had a picnic. That's when the sky began to change, and they started to worry. On the horizon, a towering bank of dark clouds appeared. They looked at each other. There was no way they could pedal fast enough to avoid the coming storm.

The girls got on their bikes and tried to head home. The weather quickly got worse. The sky was very dark, and the trees were bending in the wind. They could barely pedal against the wind. Suddenly, a yellow car pulled up alongside their bikes. Mrs. Alvarez, Maria's mother, was at the wheel. She opened a door and shouted, "Get in!" She looked frightened, too.

The girls dropped their bikes and jumped into the vehicle just as gigantic chunks of hail began to fall. The car sped down the road as hailstones bounced off the hood. Maria looked back at the dark sky and screamed, "It's a tornado!" The black funnel was chasing them! How could they outrun that monster? Ariel was terrified. It didn't look like they could escape.

Mrs. Alvarez had to shout above the roar of the storm. "Grandma's house is not far; we can make it there," she said. "I know she has a storm cellar that we can use."

She stepped on the gas and sped down the road. In a short distance, she turned sharply into a narrow driveway and screeched to a halt. Mrs. Alvarez pointed at the storm cellar doors and yelled at the girls to get inside. All three of them rushed through the doors—and not a minute too soon. A roaring sound like a freight train passed right overhead. Then, suddenly, it was over. They had made it—barely. The girls and Mrs. Alvarez exchanged a glance. Would the car still be there?

Story Elements

Every story has three elements: characters, a setting, and a plot. The plot is the problem and the way it gets resolved.

1. Before you read the story, glance at each paragraph. There are two people's names. The one you see the most is the main character. What is his name?

   _____

2. Read the story. Describe this story's setting (where and when the story happens).

   _____

3. A story's plot has two parts. The first is a conflict (problem). The second is how the problem is solved. What is the conflict in this story?

   _____

   _____

4. Is the conflict resolved? Explain.

   _____

Critical Thinking

Predict what will happen now. Will Javier become the best batter on his baseball team? Explain.

_____

_____

_____

Hero for Today

Javier is his baseball team's best pitcher because he can throw the ball fast. He throws a mean curveball, too. However, Javier is the worst hitter on his team. Every single team member hits better than he does. Everyone knows that Michael is the team's best hitter.

Today, Javier's team needs just one run to win the game. It's Michael's turn to bat, so everyone assumes he will get a home run and win the game. Michael walks up to home plate and does a practice swing. He feels confident that he can hit the ball out of the park to win. A pitch is thrown, and Michael swings and misses. "Strike one!" the umpire calls. A second pitch is thrown, and Michael misses. "Strike two!" the umpire cries. Everyone stares in disbelief when Michael swings at the last pitch and misses. Michael strikes out!

Javier groans. He is next at bat, and everyone's hopes are riding on him. If he doesn't get a hit, the game will be over, and his team will lose. Javier slowly walks to home plate with a sense of dread. He doesn't even swing at the first pitch. He swings at the second pitch and misses. Javier looks at his teammates. He hates to disappoint them. He tells himself that if he can just hit the ball and make it to first base, maybe Arnaldo, the next batter, will get a great hit.

The pitch is thrown. Javier swings and hears a crack. He hit the ball! As Javier runs to first base, he sees the ball fly over the fence. His teammates yell at him to keep going.

Javier can't believe it. He has hit a home run! The crowd cheers, and his team surrounds him after he runs across home plate. He is the hero of today's game!

Plot

Every story has a plot. The plot has two parts. The first part is a problem. The second part is the way it gets resolved.

1. Read the story. Who are Sarah and Ming?

   _____

2. Why does Ming get upset with Sarah?

   _____

   _____

3. How does Sarah react to Ming's anger?

   _____

   _____

4. What solution does Ming's father suggest?

   _____

   _____

Critical Thinking

What do you think will happen next? Explain.

_____

_____

_____

The Pencil Problem

Ming and Sarah were best friends who spent all of their time together. The girls had been friends for two years and never got into a fight, at least not until *that* day.

"Ming, may I borrow your new pencil?" Sarah asked. Ming's dad had just given her a special pink pencil with red hearts on it and a heart-shaped eraser.

"Of course! You're my best friend," answered Ming.

Sarah used the pencil for the afternoon. At the end of the school day, Ming asked for it back. Sarah looked and looked, but she could not find it!

Ming was so upset that she didn't walk home with Sarah as she always did. Instead, Ming ran home and cried. She was angry at Sarah for being so careless, and she worried that her dad would be mad, too.

The next day at school, Sarah ignored Ming. When Ming got home, her dad noticed the big frown on her face. He asked her what was wrong. Ming told him what happened and said Sarah was wrong to have lost her pencil. Her dad said that he wasn't angry and that Ming shouldn't be either! Sometimes accidents happen, even between best friends. He said, "Having a friend is more important than having a pencil."

Ming thought about what her father said. At last she realized that he was right and decided she would talk to Sarah the next day. She would ask Sarah to forgive her so they could be best friends again.

Plot

Every story has a plot. The plot has two parts. The first part is a problem. The second part is the way it gets resolved.

1. Read the story. What is Brandon's problem in the beginning?

   _____

   _____

2. Why does Brandon make a wish on a star?

   _____

   _____

3. What happens at the baseball tryouts?

   _____

   _____

4. Is Brandon's problem resolved?

   _____

Critical Thinking

How important is it for stories to have solutions? Explain.

_____

_____

_____

Wishing on a Star

Baseball tryouts were approaching. With all of the competition, Brandon realized it would be tough to make the team. The night before tryouts, Brandon went outside to do some thinking. In the night sky, he noticed what looked like a shooting star. Brandon knew it seemed foolish, but he closed his eyes and made a wish.

"Please let me make the baseball team!" he said to himself. Then Brandon laughed aloud and said, "Yeah, right. Like wishing on a star really works."

The next morning, Brandon jumped out of bed as soon as his alarm beeped. "That's strange," Brandon thought. "I don't ever feel this awake first thing in the morning." He quickly got dressed and bounded down the stairs.

"Wow," his mom said. "You're sure energetic this morning. Excited about tryouts?"

"I'm pretty nervous," Brandon said, as he devoured his waffles. "But I feel good this morning." Brandon grabbed his cleats, baseball bat, and glove and headed for the door. As he tossed his equipment in his bag, he felt his fingers tingle.

"That's weird," Brandon thought. As he ran to the park, he noticed himself picking up speed effortlessly. At the field, he sat with the other players, nervously waiting for his turn at bat. When he heard his name, he headed to home plate. His bat felt unusually light as he hoisted it over his shoulder. With the coaches watching, Brandon swung and missed the first pitch. He sighed, and then brought the bat over his shoulder again.

As the next pitch came at him, Brandon swung and made contact, sending the ball over the fence! The other players cheered and the coaches looked at each other. Brandon couldn't believe his eyes. He had never hit a ball that far.

Brandon was not sure what happened that day, but he never again doubted the power of wishing on a star.

Characters

When you read a story, it helps to think about each character. Try to picture him or her. What do you expect this person to say or do?

1. Read the story. Who are the characters?

   _____ _____ _____

   _____ _____ _____

2. What is Mrs. Gerson like?

   _____

3. Why do the boys behave the way they do after Mrs. Gerson hits the ball?

   _____

   _____

4. What do you think the team members learned from this experience?

   _____

   _____

Critical Thinking

Think about the characters in this story. Who in your own life reminds you of one of the characters? Explain.

_____

_____

_____

Mrs. Gerson's Home Run

It all started when Juan hit a home run into old Mrs. Gerson's front yard. The next thing the boys knew, Mrs. Gerson herself came ambling onto the field. She carried the baseball like it was a stinky, rotten egg.

"You boys!" she said. "I told you not to hit the ball into my yard!"

"We're sorry, Mrs. Gerson," Nick said. "Could we have our ball back?"

"Yeah, you can have it back," she said. "If you let me hit a home run." She marched to home plate and threw the ball to Ty, the pitcher. Then, she picked up a bat.

The kids looked at each other. They were unsure what to do. Mrs. Gerson stood with her feet on home plate and waved the bat around over her head. She looked like she meant what she had just said. So Ty tossed the ball toward home plate as gently as he could. Mrs. Gerson took a wild swing and somehow hit it.

"Run!" the boys shouted.

Mrs. Gerson started running toward first base as fast as she could—which was pretty slow. Lee, the catcher, walked out from behind home plate and picked up the ball. Mrs. Gerson wasn't even halfway toward first, so Lee threw the ball over the first baseman's head. Nick, the first baseman, walked as slowly as he could to get it while Mrs. Gerson approached first base.

"That way!" Juan pointed toward second. Nick threw the ball into some bushes. Ty and Andy pretended to look for it while Mrs. Gerson trudged around second, around third, and then headed home. Finally, Ty picked up the ball and threw it into the bleachers. Mrs. Gerson crossed home plate and raised her arms in victory. Everyone cheered.

"Thank you," Mrs. Gerson said as she started walking back to her house. Then she turned around. "You boys better get to work," she said. "You really need a lot of practice."

Characters

When you read a story, it helps to think about each character. Try to picture him or her. What do you expect this person to say or do?

1. Read the story. Think about Woodpecker's and Lion's actions and words. Fill in the chart below.

	Woodpecker	**Lion**
Actions		
Words		

2. What do you think Woodpecker learned from this experience?

_____

_____

Critical Thinking

Which character would you rather have as a friend? Explain.

_____

_____

_____

The Woodpecker and the Lion

from More *Jataka Tales*

Retold by Ellen C. Babbitt

One day while a lion was eating his dinner, a bone stuck in his throat. He walked up and down, up and down, roaring with fear and pain.

A woodpecker perched on a branch of a tree nearby and, hearing the lion, she kindly asked, "What is wrong with you?" The lion told the woodpecker about his trouble.

The woodpecker said, "I would take the bone out of your throat, but I do not dare to put my head into your mouth, for fear I might never get it out again. I am afraid you might eat me."

"Oh, Woodpecker, do not be afraid," the lion said. "I will not eat you. Save my life if you can!"

"I will see what I can do for you," said the woodpecker. "Open your mouth wide."

The lion did as he was told, but the woodpecker said to himself, "Who knows what this lion will do? I will be careful."

So, the woodpecker put a stick between the lion's upper and lower jaws so that he could not shut his mouth. Then the woodpecker hopped into the lion's mouth and hit the end of the bone with his beak. The second time he hit it, the bone fell out. The woodpecker hopped out of the lion's mouth and hit the stick so that it would fall out, too. The lion could now shut his mouth.

At once, the lion felt much better, but he did not say one word of thanks to the woodpecker.

One day late in the summer, the woodpecker said to the lion, "I want you to do something for me."

"Do something for you?" said the lion. "You mean you want me to do something *more* for you. I have already done a great deal for you. You cannot expect me to do anything more for you. Do not forget that once I had you in my mouth, and I let you go. That is all you can ever expect me to do for you."

The woodpecker said nothing more, but she kept away from the lion from that day on.

Title and Headings

Always read the title and headings before you read a text. They will tell you what the text will be about.

1. Read the title and headings. Based on the headings, predict what the text will be about. Fill in the chart below.

	Predictions About the Text
Taste	
Smell	
Touch	

2. Read the text. What is the purpose of the headings?

_____

_____

Critical Thinking

How do headings make this text easier to understand?

_____

_____

_____

The Flavor of Taste

Do you like to eat pizza? What about fish? Did you know that your senses of taste, smell, and touch all work together to let you identify the flavor of food?

Taste

The taste buds on our tongues detect sweet, salty, sour, and bitter tastes. Taste buds for salty flavors are near the sides and front of our tongues. Taste buds for sweet flavors are at the tips of our tongues. Bitter flavor taste buds are at the rear of our tongues. Sour taste buds are at the sides. The saliva in our mouths moistens dry foods so we can taste them.

Smell

Food smells reach specific nerves in the upper part of our noses. These nerves send messages to our brains. Any disorders that affect our sense of smell will also affect our ability to detect food flavors.

Touch

Our nose, lips, mouth, and throat react to the texture and feeling of the foods we put in our mouths. Peppermint feels cool. Jalapeños feel hot.

It's actually the combination of these three senses working together that lets us identify a flavor. And the flavor is what causes us to reject a food or to want to eat it. The flavor is the same, no matter who eats it, but we learn to like a flavor or not. Of course, we know that some flavors are liked by almost everyone—for example, chocolate! And not many kids your age really like blue cheese. Scientists do not know for sure why some foods are liked so much more than others foods.

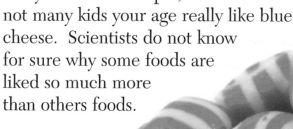

Title and Headings

Always read the title and headings before you read a text. They will tell you what the text will be about.

1. Look at the title and the headings. What will this text be about?

   _____

   _____

2. Read the text. Write each heading and two facts from that section.

Heading: _____
Fact: _____
Fact: _____
Heading: _____
Fact: _____
Fact: _____

Critical Thinking

Why did the writer use headings to divide this text into sections?

_____

_____

_____

African Art

African art has a long history. The oldest works of art are rock paintings and engravings that date back to 6000 B.C. There are many traditional types of African art. They include *textiles* and *jewelry*.

African Textiles

Africans love color, patterns, and texture. This can be seen in every type of African art. In the rainforest, the people remove bark from trees. The bark is then soaked and beaten. It is used to form fabric. This fabric is made into clothing.

The Mbuti (em-BOO-tee) women get dyes from plants. They use the dyes to paint fabrics. Sometimes fibers are dyed bright colors and then woven into cloth. The ancient Egyptians used the fibers of the flax plant. They wove its fibers into fine white cloth called *linen*.

Kente is a beautiful fabric from Ghana. First, it was made from *raffia* (dried grass). Later, it was made from silk. Kente cloth is made in long strips on a loom. The strips are then woven together. Its patterns are complex. Each pattern has a name that tells its meaning.

African Jewelry

African men, women, and children wear jewelry. The jewelry has interesting designs and may be worn on many body parts. Jewelry has special meanings in each tribe. Some jewelry is worn just on special occasions, like weddings. Other pieces, such as friendship bracelets, are given as gifts. Each piece shows the wealth and status of the owner.

Africans choose many materials for jewelry. They use fur, shells, ivory, glass, and more. Metals are also used, especially gold, tin, copper, and silver.

Typeface and Captions

A *caption* is a title or a sentence given for an illustration or a photograph. Words are set in a *typeface*. It can be normal, boldface, or italics. Sometimes words are underlined. When you see text set in one of these ways, it is a special typeface. It means the word is important.

1. Scan the text. What typeface (normal, boldface, italics) do you see?

   _____

2. Which words appear in italics?

   _____

3. Read the text. Then look at the sidebar. Why are these definitions included with the text?

   _____

4. Look at the illustration. How does the sea level caption help you to understand what the text is saying?

   _____

Critical Thinking

Write a caption that could go with the illustration box.

   _____

   _____

   _____

Earth's Tallest Mountains

Where is the "Top of the World"?

The "Top of the World" is a nickname for Mount Everest. It is the highest mountain on Earth above sea level. It stands almost 30,000 feet (8,863 m) high. It towers over the nation of Tibet in Asia.

Has anyone climbed Mount Everest?

Yes. In 1953, two climbers *summited* Mount Everest. They were Edmund Hillary and Tenzing Norgay. Since then, hundreds of climbers have reached the top. However, it is very dangerous, and dozens have died trying to do so.

What is the tallest mountain on Earth?

The tallest mountain on Earth is Mauna Kea in Hawaii. It stands on the ocean floor, and most of it is under water. It is 33,476 feet (10,203 m) from its base to its top. Although it is much taller than Mount Everest, it is not the highest mountain on Earth because so little of it appears above sea level. That is why Mount Everest is considered the world's highest mountain.

Can mountains grow?

Yes, some are growing. Rocks under the earth move and push up the mountains. In fact, each year Mount Everest grows between 2 and 4 inches (4 to 10 cm) taller. Some mountains get smaller over time due to *erosion*. Rain, snow, and ice break up the rock. As these rocks fall or wash away, the mountain loses height.

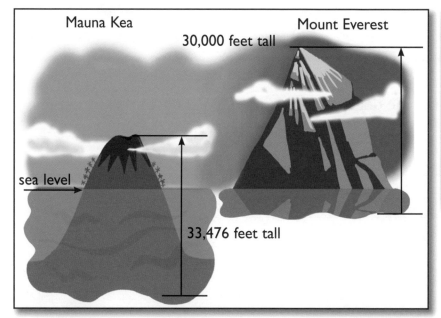

Mauna Kea

Mount Everest

30,000 feet tall

sea level

33,476 feet tall

summited—reached the top of a mountain

erosion—the process by which Earth's surface is worn away by the action of water, glaciers, and wind

Typeface and Captions

A caption is a title or a sentence given for an illustration or a photograph. Words are set in a typeface. It can be normal, boldface, or italics. Sometimes words are underlined. When you see text set in one of these ways, it is a special typeface. It means the word is important.

1. Scan the text. What special typeface is used in the text?

   _____

2. List the words set in that special typeface.

   _____

3. Read the text. Why are specific words set in a special typeface?

   _____

4. Look at the photos and captions. How do the captions help you to understand the photos?

   _____

   _____

Critical Thinking

Which of the dogs mentioned in the text have you seen in real life?

_____

_____

_____

Dog Diversity

Humans and dogs have been living together for thousands of years. During that time, humans have bred their "best friends" to specialize in many different areas. Some are bred for hunting. Others help on farms, and some help to guard people and property. Some dogs became specialists in digging up rat nests. They must be both small and good diggers. Many toy dogs are just bred to be small and cuddly and sit on people's laps!

Irish Wolfhound

The World's Tallest Dog

The tallest dog breed in the world is the *Irish Wolfhound*. They can grow up to 5 feet (1.5 m) tall at the shoulder! Wolfhounds were bred to hunt wolves. They had to be big for that job! But, these days they make wonderful, calm family pets.

English Mastiff

The World's Largest Dog

The world's largest dog is the *English Mastiff*. The largest Mastiff ever recorded was named Zorba. He weighed 343 lbs (155.6 kg) and was 8.25 feet (2.5 m) long from nose to tail! In ancient times, Mastiffs were used to fight bears and bulls. People would watch and bet money on which animal would win. Now, though, many families keep these gentle dogs as loving, protective pets.

Pekingese

The World's Smallest Dog

Some dogs are bred to be small and easily carried. In ancient China, emperors carried tiny *Pekingese* dogs in the sleeves of their robes! Today, the smallest breeds are the *Chihuahua* and the *Yorkshire Terrier* (Yorkie). The current record for the smallest dog alive goes to a Chihuahua named Heaven Sent Brandy. She was only 6 inches (15.2 cm) from nose to tail. The smallest dog ever recorded in history is a Yorkie named Sylvia. She was just 2.5 inches (6.4 cm) tall at the shoulder, 3.5 inches (8.9 cm) long and weighed only 4 ounces (113.4 g)!

Yorkshire Terrier

Graphics

Always look at the pictures, maps, or diagrams before you read a text. They will give you clues as to what the text will be about.

1. Preview the text. Look at the illustrations. What is shown in the top illustration?

    _____

    _____

2. What is shown in the illustration on the bottom?

    _____

    _____

3. Read the text. Why was one fact singled out and put in a sidebar?

    _____

    _____

Critical Thinking

Would you have been able to draw a diagram of the eye if you had only this text without its graphics? Explain.

_____

_____

_____

SIGHT

Sight lets you see the world around you. Eyesight is one of the most important ways people get along in the world. Have you ever worn a blindfold? If so, then, you know how challenging it is to be without sight even for a few minutes.

Your eye is an amazing structure. Most of your eyeball is *vitreous humor*, which is a clear, gelatin-like substance. The white part of your eye is called the *sclera*. This is a coating that covers most of the eyeball. The *cornea* is part of the sclera. The cornea, which is clear, covers the colored part of your eye. The cornea is like a window that lets light into your eyeball.

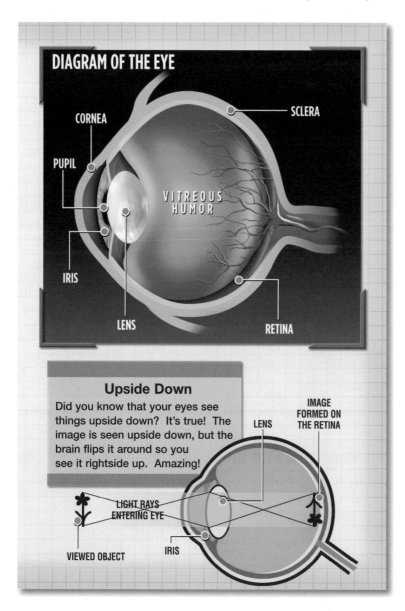

DIAGRAM OF THE EYE

CORNEA
SCLERA
PUPIL
VITREOUS HUMOR
IRIS
LENS
RETINA

Upside Down

Did you know that your eyes see things upside down? It's true! The image is seen upside down, but the brain flips it around so you see it rightside up. Amazing!

LENS
IMAGE FORMED ON THE RETINA
LIGHT RAYS ENTERING EYE
VIEWED OBJECT
IRIS

The *pupil* and the *iris* lie behind the cornea. The pupil is the black circle you see in the center of your eye, and the iris is the colored circle around it. Your iris controls the amount of light that comes through your pupil. When it is dark, the iris makes the pupil bigger to let in more light. When there is bright light, the iris makes your pupil smaller to let in less light.

The light that enters your eye then reaches the *lens*. The lens focuses the image onto the *retina*, which is on the back of your eyeball. The retina sends a message to your brain, and the brain tells you what you are seeing.

Graphics

Always look at the pictures, maps, or diagrams before you read a text. They will give you clues as to what the text will be about.

1. Preview the text. Look at the diagram. What does it show?

    _____

2. Read the text. How does it help you to understand the diagram better?

    _____

    _____

3. Use the diagram to answer the next three questions:

    What happens to the water in lakes and oceans?

    _____

    How does water move from a lake to the ocean?

    _____

    Where does evaporated water go?

    _____

Critical Thinking

How did the diagram work with the text to help you to understand how deserts form?

_____

_____

_____

Deserts

What Is a Desert?

A desert is an area of land with very little rain and, most of the time, high temperatures during the day.

In a desert, less than 10 inches (25.4 cm) of rain falls each year. The ground is usually dry. Whenever it does rain in a desert, the heat of the sun dries up most of the water again. This is called *evaporation*.

One reason for this evaporation is the extreme high temperatures. During the day, the ground soaks up the heat. The temperature in the desert can reach as high as 130°F (54°C). How hot is that? Most people are comfortable at about 70°F (21°C). Deserts can get almost twice that hot! Yet desert nights can be very cold. The ground releases its heat at night.

How Does a Desert Form?

Many deserts form due to mountain ranges. The tall mountains prevent moisture from getting past them. *Precipitation* (rain and snow) falls on one side of the mountain range, but the air is dry by the time it gets to the other side. That's where the desert is located.

Some deserts form because they are far away from bodies of water. The clouds soak up moisture from lakes and oceans, but then they drop the water long before they get to the desert. The clouds just do not travel as far as the desert.

How Water Moves Through the Environment

PRECIPITATION   EVAPORATION   EVAPORATION

Desert   Lake   River   Land   Ocean

Topic Sentences

A topic sentence is one that sums up what the paragraph is about. It can appear anywhere in the paragraph, but it is often is the first sentence.

1. Read the text. Write the topic sentence of the first paragraph.

   _____

   _____

2. Write the topic sentence of the second paragraph.

   _____

3. Write the topic sentence of the third paragraph.

   _____

4. Write the topic sentence of the fourth paragraph.

   _____

   _____

Critical Thinking

How can the topic sentences of each paragraph help you summarize this text?

_____

_____

_____

An Amazing Planet

Saturn, the sixth planet from the sun, is the second-largest planet in our solar system. It is at least nine times bigger than Earth. Its winds can blow up to 1,100 miles per hour (1,770 kph), which is much, much faster than our fastest jet plane.

Saturn does not have a solid surface. Its outer layers are made of gases. Although the inside of the planet is made of rock, that rock is covered by more gas.

Since Saturn is gaseous instead of solid, its shape is pliable. Plus, it rotates on its axis so fast that the force squashes it into a fat pancake shape. Saturn is the least round of all the planets.

Perhaps the most amazing thing about Saturn is the rings that surround it. These rings are mostly made up of dust specks and ice chunks. Some of the ice chunks are almost as big as a house! Others are as small as tiny pieces of sand. Galileo first saw Saturn's rings in 1610. Saturn also has 62 moons orbiting it.

Topic Sentences

A *topic sentence is one that sums up what the paragraph is about. It can appear anywhere in the paragraph, but it is often is the first sentence.*

1. Read the text. What is the topic sentence for the second paragraph?

    _____

2. What is the topic sentence for the third paragraph?

    _____

    _____

3. How do the topic sentences help you to know what each paragraph will be about?

    _____

    _____

Critical Thinking

How can you use what you know about topic sentences the next time you read a nonfiction text?

_____

_____

_____

Aarrgg! Pirates!

For many years, pirates have appeared in movies and books as daring men of action. Pirate stories often tell a tale of people who were mistreated. They were forced to become pirates. Their lives seem almost heroic. But this was rarely true.

Pirates went by different names. *Privateers* were pirates from countries in Europe. These ships and crews were hired by one country to rob the ships of another country. *Corsairs* were pirates from North African countries. They attacked ships, and kidnapped the crews and held them in jail. For a long time, most countries paid money to get their sailors back. *Buccaneers* sailed the West Indies and Caribbean Sea. They were the worst of the pirates. They sometimes killed the whole crew even after the men surrendered.

Since it was thought to be unlucky to have a woman aboard a ship, there were few female pirates. One was Ching Shih of China. She led a force of 80,000 pirates, known as the Red Flag Fleet. Anne Bonny and Mary Read were two famous women pirates. They raided ships in the Caribbean Sea. Both were strong fighters. They survived many battles.

Songs, plays, and novels have been written about pirates who sailed the seven seas. Piracy reached its height in the 1700s. Yet the end was coming. The countries of the world got together to stop piracy. Many countries stopped encouraging their sailors to attack other countries' ships. Countries stopped paying ransom for kidnapped crews. Instead, they sent their navies to attack the countries holding their sailors. Pirates were caught and tried in court and severely punished. By 1850, piracy was no longer a major problem on the high seas.

Main Idea

The main idea is what a text is mostly about. In nonfiction text, the main idea may be stated in a sentence. For some fictional texts, you will have to think to determine the main ideas.

1. Read the text. The overall main idea is not stated. You will have to figure it out. Write it below.

   _____

   _____

2. Find six details that are the most important to supporting the main idea. Write them below.

   _____

   _____

   _____

   _____

   _____

   _____

Critical Thinking

How did thinking about the main idea of each paragraph help you understand the overall main idea of the text?

_____

_____

_____

Guide Dogs

Have you seen large dogs in stores or restaurants and wondered why they were there? Those dogs are probably guide dogs. Because guide dogs are so well trained, they are welcome everywhere.

Who Uses a Guide Dog?

People who are blind may use guide dogs called seeing-eye dogs. These special dogs help people get around. They help them do everyday things such as cross a street. Some people who have hearing problems have hearing-ear dogs. These dogs let their owners know when an alarm clock rings, a smoke detector goes off, or the doorbell rings.

What Do Guide Dogs Do?

Guide dogs learn to wear a harness on their backs. Their owner holds onto it. The dogs learn what words such as "left" and "right" mean. They learn never to take their owner into moving traffic.

Volunteers spend months training each guide dog. Then the dog spends one month working with its future owner. At that time, the owner and dog get to know one another as they train together.

How Should You Treat a Guide Dog?

Do not pet a guide dog when it is wearing its harness. Always ask the owner's permission before interacting with the dog, and don't be upset if the person says no. Someone who is blind depends completely on the dog to do its job without any distractions. If the owner approves, you may stroke the dog's shoulder area. Do not pat the dog on its head.

You should never give the guide dog commands. Only his or her owner can do so. And don't try to hold the dog's harness or steer the person while the dog is guiding the owner.

Main Idea

The main idea is what a text is mostly about. In nonfiction text, the main idea may be stated in a sentence. For some fictional texts, you will have to think to determine the main ideas.

1. Read the story. Then write the main idea in the center of the graphic organizer below.

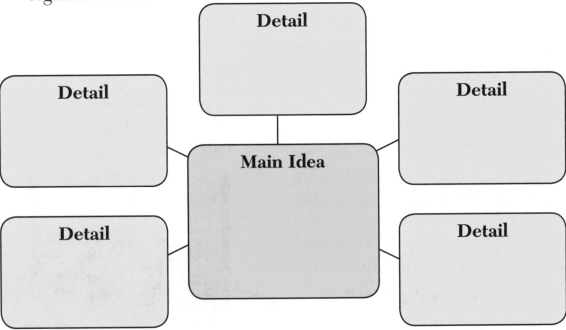

2. Details support the main idea. Find five important details in the story. Write one inside each section of the graphic organizer.

Critical Thinking

How does finding the main idea of a fiction story differ from finding the main idea of a nonfiction text?

_____

_____

_____

An Unusual Invention

Squeak, whir, chunk-chunk-a-chunk! The strange looking machine sprang to life. Joshua's heart skipped a beat. "It works! It really works!" he exclaimed.

"We don't know that. And we won't know it until we test it," replied Genevieve. She was Joshua's boss and the chief inventor on this project. "Let's try running the full sequence with a box of cookies. Grab those Chocolate Chip Munchies over there and put them on the departure pad."

Joshua followed her instructions. Genevieve adjusted some dials and typed a code on her wireless keyboard. "Ignition in 3, 2, 1," she said. Suddenly, a bright light flashed. The green and brown writing on the cookie box twinkled and began to fade. In a moment, the whole box vanished! Joshua held his breath and turned to look at another portion of the machine.

Genevieve flipped a switch. "Arrival in 3, 2, 1," she whispered. Nothing happened. Joshua exhaled slowly. Genevieve furrowed her brow. Then she started to laugh.

"Of course," she cried out, "I almost forgot!" She quickly typed another code on her keyboard. Instantly, a shimmer appeared across the room in the portion of the machine they had been watching. Slowly the outline of a box became visible. The green and brown letters reappeared. It took almost a full minute, but eventually the entire box emerged from thin air.

Joshua gave a whoop, and Genevieve's face broke into a wide grin. She walked over to the box, opened the lid, and popped a cookie into her mouth. Then she offered the box to Joshua. "So, my fellow inventor, how would you like a taste of the world's first teleported cookies?"

Details

As you read, ask yourself, "What is this text about?" That is the main idea. Then you can find the details that support the main idea.

1. Read the story. What is the main idea? Write it in the top bar below.

Main Idea
Detail
Detail
Detail
Detail
Detail

2. Details tell more about the main idea. Write five important details in the chart above.

Critical Thinking

Do you think it is easier to find the main idea and details in a fictional story or a nonfiction text? Explain.

_____

_____

_____

The Light at the End of the Tunnel

"Which way should we turn now?" asked Mario. His soft voice sounded like a shout in the still silence of the cave. It startled Leah. She stopped and looked down at her map. "We need to keep going west," she replied. "It shouldn't be much further now."

The ceiling had gotten lower, and the two tired spelunkers were now forced to crawl along the cold, clammy floor.

"I don't know how you talked me into this adventure," Mario moaned. He was dirty, hungry, and cranky. With some effort, he struggled to squeeze his large frame through the most narrow part of the tunnel's opening. Then he looked up and gasped. Leah was standing in front of him and had switched off her lantern. Mario did the same.

The entire chamber was bathed in a soft, silver glow. In the very center of the cavern was a chimney-like opening that allowed light from the full moon and star-clustered sky to filter in. That was not the only source of illumination. Embedded in the walls were small, luminous crystals. It looked as if someone had attached diamonds to a set of outdoor lights and strung them throughout the cave. Columns of colorful rock reached from the floor to the ceiling. It no longer seemed like a cave. It looked like a magical fairyland.

Mario suddenly remembered to close his gaping mouth. Leah's smile beamed up at him. "So, do you think it was worth it?" she whispered.

"I can't think of anything in my life that has ever been more worth the trouble!" Mario cried in amazement. The two friends sat quietly in the beautiful cave for a long time. Then, without a word, the pair turned and started the long, hard journey back home.

Details

As you read, ask yourself, "What is this text about?" That is the main idea. Then you can find the details that support the main idea.

1. Read the text. Write the main idea in the center of the graphic organizer below.

2. Write details to support the main idea. Write one detail in each box of the graphic organizer.

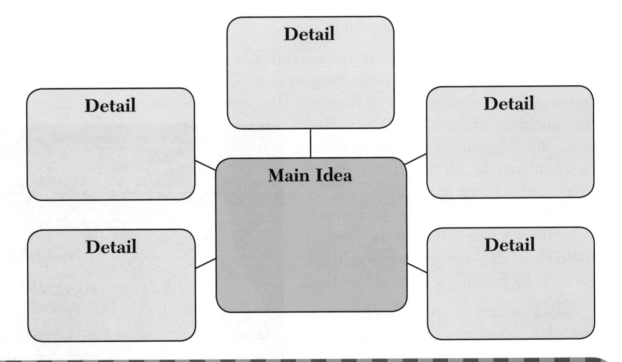

Critical Thinking

How do the details in a fiction story differ from the details in a nonfiction text? Explain.

_____

_____

_____

How Animals "Talk"

Humans communicate with one another all the time. We talk, phone, write, and email. But animals can't do any of these things. How do they communicate?

We've all heard dogs growl and bark and cats meow and purr. Making sounds is the most common form of animal "talk." Dogs make sounds when they're scared, happy, or angry. They make sounds to warn you. Gorillas and beavers make throaty sounds. Some animals, such as grasshoppers, make sounds by rubbing their legs together.

Other animals communicate through marking. Black bears mark their territory by biting and clawing trees. Other kinds of marking include deer scratching their horns on a tree trunk or foxes spraying urine on a bush.

Some animals watch for clues from other members of their species. Honeybees dance to show others in their hive where a new food source is located. Electric eels and lightning bugs flash lights to send signals to mates. Dogs bow to let other dogs know they want to play.

Scent is a way that animals communicate, too. Certain female animals send out smells that attract males. And none of us wants to be around when a skunk feels threatened!

Some animals "get physical" to communicate. For example, wolves wrestle to figure out their rank in the pack.

honeybees   **cat**   **grasshopper**   **dog**

Main Idea and Details

When you read, decide what the text is mostly about. That is the main idea. The main idea is supported by details. Some of the details are important. Others are not so important.

1. Read the text. Write the main idea of each paragraph in the graphic organizer below.

2. Write one important detail for each main idea.

Main Idea	Detail
Paragraph 1:	
Paragraph 2:	
Paragraph 3:	
Paragraph 4:	

Critical Thinking

How did you decide which details to include and which to eliminate?

_____

_____

_____

Newton's Laws of Motion

Isaac Newton is a famous scientist. He explained three laws about objects and the forces that act upon them. They are called Newton's Laws of Motion.

First Law of Motion

Newton's First Law of Motion concerns *inertia*. Inertia resists changes in motion. The law states that until another force acts upon the object, the object will keep doing what it's already doing. This applies whether the object is sitting still or moving. Objects that are still will remain still. Objects that are moving continue moving in the same direction at a constant speed. However, the force called *friction* will make an object slow down and eventually stop.

Second Law of Motion

Newton's Second Law of Motion concerns *acceleration*. It tells what happens when a force is applied to an object. It says that the greater the force, the more the object accelerates, or speeds up. The object will move in the same direction as the force that acts upon it. A golf ball will fly through the air in the same direction as the golf club that hit it. A stronger force is needed to make a heavier object accelerate at the same speed as a lightweight object. This makes sense. For example, it takes more strength to throw a bowling ball than a golf ball.

Third Law of Motion

Newton's Third Law of Motion describes *action* and *reaction*. It says that for every action, there is an equal and opposite reaction. Whenever a force pushes on an object, the object pushes back. The force of the object pushing back is the *reaction force*. This is why a rowboat moves when oarsmen row. The oarsmen push backward on the water with the oars. The water pushes back on the oars with an equal and opposite force. This moves the boat forward. This law explains why a chair sits on the floor instead of falling through it. The weight of the chair pushes down on the floor. The floor pushes up against the chair and holds it there.

Chronological Order

Putting events in the order in which they occur is called chronological order. It gives the events from start to finish. It is a good way to organize what happens in a text.

1. Read the text. Number the sentences in the correct order from 1 to 5.

    _____ Hatshepsut made herself the pharaoh.

    _____ Hatshepsut served as the regent for Thutmose II.

    _____ Thutmose III became an infant pharaoh.

    _____ Thutmose II died.

    _____ Thutmose I was pharaoh.

2. On the time line, write the event that occurred for each date. Not all dates are in the text; you must figure some of them out for yourself.

1518 B.C.	1504 B.C.	1497 B.C.	1458 B.C.

Critical Thinking

Why do authors write events in chronological order?

_____

_____

_____

Hatshepsut, the Female Pharaoh

Many people have called Hatshepsut "the great woman" in Egypt's history. She lived during a time called the New Kingdom. Before her time, no woman had ever ruled Egypt.

About 1518 B.C., Thutmose I became the pharaoh and took the throne in Egypt. He and his queen had two sons and two daughters. However, just one child lived to adulthood. Her name was Hatshepsut. When she was a teenager, her father died.

Hatshepsut was a strong young woman who wanted to lead others. She could read and write. She liked to learn new things. And she had watched her father while he ruled as pharaoh. Hatshepsut had her own ideas about how to make Egypt great.

Thutmose I had another son with another wife. So, Thutmose II became the new pharaoh. Since he was just eight years old, Hatshepsut acted as his *regent* for 10 years. A regent is a person who rules while the pharaoh is too young or ill. Hatshepsut was strong willed and smart. She made most of the decisions about the nation. The priests and other leaders of Egypt followed her advice.

Thutmose II died young. In about 1504 B.C., Thutmose III became pharaoh. But he was just a baby. Again, Hatshepsut served as the regent. After about seven years, Hatshepsut made herself pharaoh. She remained the pharaoh for 22 years. This means that she ruled the most powerful civilization of her time. She died in 1458 B.C.

Chronological Order

Putting events in the order in which they occur is called chronological order. It gives the events from start to finish. It is a good way to organize what happens in a text.

1. Read the text. Number the sentences in the correct order from 1–5.

   _____ The oyster is put into a cage and lowered into the ocean.

   _____ The oyster creates a pearl.

   _____ A worker inserts a tiny bead into an oyster shell.

   _____ The pearl is used in a ring, an earring, or a necklace.

   _____ A worker removes the oyster from the ocean and removes its pearl.

2. How is it helpful to have this text written in chronological order?

   _____

   _____

Critical Thinking

There are white pearls and black pearls. Do you think the process to form each kind is the same? Explain.

   _____

   _____

   _____

Gem From a Tiny Grain of Sand

Have you ever seen a pearl necklace? You should know how hard it is for each of those pearls to be made!

Pearls form in special kinds of oysters. An oyster is a sea animal that lives in a shell, which means it's a type of shellfish. The inside of an oyster's shell is lined with nacre. This lining is also called the pearly layer. It is shiny like a pearl.

Sometimes a grain of sand gets inside an oyster's shell. The oyster has a natural defense mechanism to prevent a potentially threatening parasite from living inside its shell. That defense is to seal off the irritant by growing layers of nacre around the object. Over time, as the grain of sand gets covered with layers of nacre, it forms a pearl! Only certain kinds of oysters create beautiful, shiny pearls, and most of them live in tropical seas. In the past, people dove into the water and killed hundreds of oysters just to find a few pearls to use in jewelry.

Pearls may come in many strange shapes; they are not all round. For use in jewelry, most pearls are round. Today, making pearls is not left up to nature. Instead, people create cultured pearls at sea farms. Trained workers put a tiny bead into each oyster shell. Then they put the oysters into cages and lower them into the ocean. The more time that passes, the larger the pearl gets. Some pearls are retrieved after six months, and others are retrieved after three years.

Logical Order

Logical order is putting information in an order that makes sense. For example, you would tell what you plan to do on a weekend in the order in which you think you will do it.

Scan the list of parts to answer the first three questions:

1. How many tubes of wood glue should be in the kit? _____

2. How many perches should be in the kit? _____

3. How many roof pieces should be in the kit? _____

4. Read the text. After which step must you let the glue dry?

   _____

5. What should you do if your kit is missing any of the parts?

   _____

   _____

Critical Thinking

If you wanted to stain or paint your birdhouse, where would that step go in the sequence above?

_____

_____

_____

Build Your Own Birdhouse

Parts in the Kit:

- 2 roof pieces
- 2 side pieces
- 1 front piece, with pointed top and two holes
- 1 end piece, with pointed top
- 1 floor piece
- 1 round perch
- 1 metal chain with two wood screws
- 1 tube of wood glue

Directions:

1. Place the floor piece flat. Glue the two side pieces to it at a 90-degree angle.

2. Glue the front and end pieces to the three pieces.

3. Glue the two roof pieces in place. Let the birdhouse sit overnight or until the glue is dry.

4. Push the round perch into the small hole on the front of the birdhouse.

5. Fasten the metal chain to the roof by putting the wood screws in the two predrilled holes.

6. Now, find a secluded spot on a tree branch or under the eaves of your roof. Hang your birdhouse.

Soon, you will have a family of birds nesting there. You'll be able to spend hours watching them.

If any part is missing, please call 1-888-000-9876 between 8 A.M. and 5 P.M. Monday–Friday to get a replacement.

You can hang your birdhouse on a tree.

A baby tree swallow calls for food.

A mother tree swallow visits her baby in a birdhouse.

Logical Order

Logical order is putting information in an order that makes sense. For example, you would tell what you plan to do on a weekend in the order in which you think you will do it.

1. Read the text. This text has sequence words that help to tell you the order in which to do things. Write the four sequence words below.

   _____ _____ _____ _____

2. Write the five important steps to create a budget.

   1. _____

   2. _____

   3. _____

   4. _____

   5. _____

3. What happens if Sari earns less than she wants to spend?

   _____

   _____

Critical Thinking

Where might Sari keep the money that she saves?

_____

_____

_____

How to Make a Simple Budget

Learning to live within a budget is an important part of growing up. Let's look at a simple budget. Sari gets an allowance of $5.00 per week. She also earns $15.50 per week helping Ms. Liu, her neighbor, weed her garden. Both amounts are her income. Adding them together results in her total income.

Sari's expenses include $9.50 per week for a movie ticket and $5.00 per week for eating out. Adding these together gives her total expenses. At the end of each week, Sari has $6.00 left after her expenses. She puts this $6.00 in her savings. Sari is doing a good job at living within her budget! So, can you make a budget?

First, keep track of your income and expenses, just like Sari did. Start by writing in a notebook what you earn and spend. This helps you to keep track of your money each week.

Next, you need to make a plan. What do you want to save for—video games, DVDs, gifts for others? Once you know, you can plan for the weeks ahead.

Under the heading *Income*, make a list of what you will earn. This might

Sari's Weekly Budget

Income
Allowance $5.00
Helping neighbor $15.50
Total income **$20.50**

Expenses
Movie ticket $9.50
Eating out $5.00
Total expenses **$14.50**

Total income – total expenses = $6.00 savings

include your allowance or money from extra chores. Add up all the things in your Income list. This will be your total income.

Then make a list under the heading *Expenses*. Write the things on which you expect to spend your money. This might include snacks, movies, CDs—it's up to you! Add up all the things in your Expenses list to get your total expenses. Finally, subtract your total expenses from your total income. This will tell you how much money you'll have left at the end of the week. That money can go into your savings.

Fact and Opinion

1. Read the text. Write a fact given by Mr. Skippy.

   _____

2. Write an opinion given by Shay.

   _____

3. Read each statement. Write *F* for Fact or *O* for Opinion.

   _____ The buttons on the controller were difficult to push.

   _____ Students tell Mr. Skippy what they think about the video game.

   _____ "The game crashed on me three times while I was playing," said Sheila.

   _____ *Pig Planet Nine* uses three colors in its graphics.

   _____ *Pig Planet Nine* has too many bugs.

Critical Thinking

After reading this, would you like to play *Pig Planet Nine*? Explain why or why not.

_____

_____

_____

Pig Planet Nine

"All right, students," Mr. Skippy began, "Now that you have had a chance to play the game, we at Happy Fun Games, Inc. would like to know what you think about it!"

Shay raised her hand. "I think that it is the best game that I have ever played!" she exclaimed.

Joey frowned and said, "It had a pig as a main character. Pigs are physically incapable of doing most of the moves. For instance, a pig could not leap from the ground up into a spaceship orbiting the planet! It is too unrealistic."

"I thought that the art was especially good," offered Omar, "although I was a little surprised that it only used three colors. I think it could be improved if they used more than just red, white, and black."

"This is good feedback. Does anyone have anything else they would like to add?"

"The buttons on the controller were difficult to push. I found that frustrating!" exclaimed Mariah.

"I thought the buttons were just fine," argued Will.

"Well, my hands are smaller than yours. Maybe that is why it was more difficult for me," Mariah observed.

"The game crashed on me three times while I was playing," said Sheila. "It has too many bugs!"

"Yes, but it really was exciting! I think that once you get all the bugs fixed, it will be a really great game!" Shay said enthusiastically.

Mr. Skippy typed furiously on his laptop to record what the students were saying. "Well, thank you very much, everyone! I will bring these notes back to the team. We really appreciate your help. As soon as we complete it, I will make sure that each one of you gets a free copy of *Pig Planet Nine* so that you all can play!"

Fact and Opinion

A fact is something that can be proven. An opinion is what someone thinks. Today is rainy is a fact. You can prove it by looking outside. Rainy days are wonderful is an opinion. Not everyone would agree!

1. Read the text. Write one fact given in the first paragraph.

    _____

2. Write the opinion given in the second paragraph.

    _____

3. Read each statement below. Write *F* for Fact or *O* for Opinion.

    _____ Michael Jordan has 6 championship rings, and he won Finals MVP each of those years.

    _____ Kareem Abdul-Jabbar earned over 38,000 points in his career.

    _____ No other basketball player can come close to being as amazing as Michael Jordan.

    _____ Michael Jordan was a ball hog.

    _____ Wilt Chamberlain scored 100 points in a single game.

Critical Thinking

Think of a time when you argued with someone over who or what was "the best." Briefly tell about it.

_____

_____

_____

BASKETBALL GREATS

Brian and Tabitha usually agreed on everything. They liked the same favorite food (pizza), the same favorite color (yellow), and the same favorite video game (*Zambu, Warrior Queen*). This made it all the more upsetting for Tabitha to realize how much of a dunderhead Brian could be!

"Michael Jordan? Are you kidding me? Everyone knows that Kobe Bryant is the best basketball player who has ever lived!" she exclaimed.

"No way!" countered Brian. "Michael Jordan has six championship rings. And he won Finals MVP every one of those years. No other basketball player can even come close to being that amazing!"

"Michael Jordan was a ball hog," insisted Tabitha. "He was lucky to have a team that helped him get all the way to the finals that many times! Kobe is a team player. He just didn't have the team he needed to get as many rings as MJ!" She was really starting to fume now.

Just then, Tabitha's mother came in from the other room. "You know," she said, "you both have some really good points. But, I wonder if the two of you know about the other great basketball players."

"Who do you mean, Mom?" asked Tabitha.

"Well, did you know that Kareem Abdul-Jabbar scored over 38,000 points in his career? And Wilt Chamberlain once scored 100 points in a single game?" asked Tabitha's mom.

"100 points! Are you serious? I wish I had seen that!" Brian said.

"Yes, it's true. He even averaged over 50 points a game during the 1961–1962 season."

"Wow! I didn't know that," said Tabitha thoughtfully. "Hey, Brian, I have an idea."

"I bet it is the same one I have!" Brian replied, smiling.

"Let's do some research!" they said together and laughed.

Proposition and Support

A proposition is a writer's opinion. The writer wants the reader to agree. So the writer gives support (reasons and information) to get the reader to share the same opinion.

1. Read the title. What do you think the writer's proposition will be?

   _____

   _____

2. Read the text. Why was the traditional school year calendar developed?

   _____

   _____

3. Write at least three details that support the writer's proposition.

   _____

   _____

   _____

Critical Thinking

State an argument against year-round school.

_____

_____

_____

Let's Have Year-Round School

Summer vacation from school is too long. Students have to review everything in the fall when they come back to school. They have to re-adjust to the school schedule.

The traditional school year calendar was created when many people lived on farms. Students had the summer off so they could help with the harvesting. Today, most people do not live on farms. They do not need the whole summer off.

I propose that there should be more year-round schools. In this model, school vacations happen throughout the year. Students are still in school for the same amount of time. The vacation schedule is just spread out throughout the year. Instead of two months off in the summer, there may only be one month off. Students could still go to summer camp and have a summer vacation. Students and teachers would feel less burned out during the school year because their vacations would be spread out.

The research is mixed about whether year-round schools improve student achievement. Some studies show improvement whereas others do not. Despite this, I still think the year-round school is a better model. I think it can help with the problem of the long summer vacation.

Proposition and Support

A proposition is a writer's opinion. The writer wants the reader to agree. So the writer gives support (reasons and information) to get the reader to share the same opinion.

1. Read the text. Then fill in the chart below.

Position 1: T. rex was a	Position 2: T. rex was a
Support:	Support:

2. In your opinion, which position has more support? Explain.

_____

_____

Critical Thinking

How is proposition and support similar to a writer stating a problem and offering a solution?

_____

_____

_____

THE GREAT T. REX DEBATE

We are studying dinosaurs in science class. Today, my teacher, Mr. Chase, asked if we thought that Tyrannosaurus rex (T. rex) was a predator that hunted live prey or a scavenger that just ate dead animals. He divided the class into two groups.

My half of the class had to show that T. rex was a scavenger. By doing some research on the Internet, we learned that scientists have found some evidence that the T. rex was better suited to scavenging. T. rex had very tiny arms, which would not have been helpful in hunting. It was also a very big dinosaur, and may have been too heavy to run very fast, kind of like today's elephants. Its legs were built for walking long distances, which scavengers have to do to find food. Another important thing for a scavenger to have is a good sense of smell. The part of T. rex's brain that picked up scent was especially large.

The other half of the class presented their evidence for T. rex being a predator. They showed that T. rex's bones were very thick and heavy, which might mean that it could move rapidly to capture prey. Also, its small arms would not have been needed to catch food. Sharks and eagles do not have any arms, yet both are very good predators. There have also been fossils found with what looks like T. rex tooth marks on dinosaur bones.

After both sides presented their evidence, we asked Mr. Chase which side was right. He said that both groups might be right. Scientists do not know for sure whether T. rex was a hunter or a scavenger. And some of today's predators, like lions, are both. So, until scientists can find more evidence, we might all be correct!

Author's Purpose

When you read, ask yourself why the author wrote the text. Read carefully to determine the author's view about the topic.

1. Read the text. Why did the author write this text?

   _____

   _____

2. In this text, the important details tell what, when, and where. Write them below.

   What: _____

   When: _____

   Where: _____

3. What does the author hope you will do as a result of reading this text?

   _____

   _____

Critical Thinking

What does this text remind you of? Explain.

_____

_____

_____

Come to Our Class Play!

Mr. Peyton's fourth-grade class invites you to come to its first play of the school year, *A Husband for Mama*. It will be presented in the school auditorium at 2 P.M. this Friday. The play is only about 30 minutes long. Nobody will miss the bus.

The play is a comedy set in the year 1932. Anita Lopez plays the starring role of the widowed mother. She wants to get her three daughters married and out of the house. However, her daughters are not pleased with the fellows she has chosen for them. The sisters decide to find a husband for their mother, so she will leave them alone. That is when the fun begins!

Fourth grader Robert Stanowicz directed the play. The whole class worked together to create terrific costumes and scenery. Don't miss this play, which promises to be a lot of fun. We guarantee you'll laugh a lot!

There will be cookies and punch served right after the play. So be smart and be there!

Author's Purpose

When you read, ask yourself why the author wrote the text.
Read carefully to determine the author's view about the topic.

1. Read the text. Why did the author write this text?

   _____

   _____

2. How does the author feel about giving things away to charity? How do
   you know?

   _____

   _____

3. What is a benefit that the kids discover from giving away their stuff?

   _____

   _____

   _____

Critical Thinking

Would you ever shop at a thrift store? Explain.

   _____

   _____

   _____

Giving Stuff Away

Chris and Molly ran into the house just as it began to storm. Their mom had seen on the news that it was supposed to rain all day, so she asked the two kids to gather up all the clothes that no longer fit them and put them into a box. Tomorrow, they would donate the clothes to charity.

Chris and Molly wondered why they didn't just have a yard sale and sell all their old stuff. Their mom explained that it was good to donate. She said that the thrift stores sell the contributions and then use the money to help needy people.

Chris went through his dresser, pulling out all the jeans, shorts, and shirts that he had outgrown. Then he started on his closet. A few sweaters, some dress pants and dress shirts, a jacket, and some shoes all went into the give-away box.

Molly pulled out a dress, some pants, several sweaters, and some shirts, all of which were too small for her. She found a hat she had forgotten about, too.

Soon the kids discovered it was fun to think about what to give away. They started going through their old toys, books, games, dolls, and stuffed animals. They pulled out everything they didn't use anymore.

When they finished, Chris and Molly had enough things to fill up three big boxes! Their mom helped them to load the boxes into the back of the SUV. The kids felt good because they were helping people. Plus, their rooms were no longer cluttered!

Compare and Contrast

When you compare, you ask yourself how things are the same.
When you contrast, you focus on how things are different.

1. Read the text. Then complete the chart to compare and contrast baseball with softball and slow-pitch with fast-pitch softball.

Baseball	Softball
uses a smaller, harder ball	
	seven innings in a game
uses a bat, a ball, bases, and gloves	
overhand pitches	
	has a smaller playing field
Slow-pitch Softball	**Fast-pitch Softball**
ball is thrown slowly	
	nine players on a team

2. Which would you prefer to play: baseball or softball? Explain.

_____

_____

Critical Thinking

Are baseball and softball more alike or different? Explain.

_____

_____

_____

Softball Is Not Baseball

It might look like baseball, and it might sound like baseball, but softball is not baseball. It is a completely different sport! How can that be? After all, the two sports use the same gear: a bat, a ball, three bases, and gloves. However, things are done differently in the two games.

A softball game has seven innings, while a baseball game has nine. The softball field is smaller than a baseball field. A softball is bigger and softer than a baseball. In softball, pitchers throw the ball underhand. In baseball, they throw it overhand.

There are even two kinds of softball: slow pitch and fast pitch. A slow-pitch team has 10 players. A fast-pitch team has nine. In fast pitch, pitchers throw the ball fast, and players can bunt the ball and steal bases. Slow-pitch balls can be smaller than the fast-pitch balls.

Softball started in Chicago in 1887 as an indoor game. Later it was played outdoors.

Have you ever played softball? Give it a try!

Compare and Contrast

When you compare, you ask yourself how things are the same.
When you contrast, you focus on how things are different.

1. Read the text. Compare and contrast soccer and basketball below.

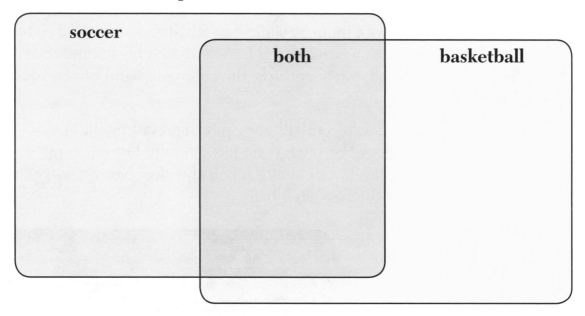

soccer

both

basketball

2. Which sport would you rather play: soccer or basketball? Why?

_____

_____

Critical Thinking

What do you think is the most popular sport in your nation?
Why do you think so?

_____

_____

_____

A Soccer Ball and a Basketball Have a Talk

The sporting goods store was closed, and the customers and employees were gone for the day. A basketball and a soccer ball sat on the shelf next to each other. They began talking.

"I sure hope a nice kid takes me home," said the soccer ball.

"I hope I find a loving home, too," echoed the basketball.

The soccer ball responded, "I'll bet I get picked before you. Soccer is more popular than basketball. Soccer is played around the world."

The basketball became defensive and said, "Well, basketball is popular, too. It's even played in the Olympics!"

"So is soccer! And it's a better sport," retorted the soccer ball.

Neither one spoke for a while. Then the basketball said, "I see we're both round and full of air. How else are we similar?"

"Well…," said the soccer ball, "I play with two teams on an outdoor field. Players use their feet to dribble and kick me to pass me to other players. Sometimes they hit me with their heads. Points are made when I pass through a goal."

The basketball thought a minute and then said, "I also play with two teams. Players use their hands to dribble or throw me, but no kicking or head butting allowed! We play on a court. To score points, they throw me through a hoop." Then the basketball added, "There are five players on each team."

The soccer ball boasted, "I told you soccer is better. It has ELEVEN players on each team."

The basketball said, "Look, we can't keep arguing like this. No one will take us home."

"I guess you're right," said the soccer ball.

"OK, let's both agree that our sports are popular. We help players develop their minds and bodies so they learn teamwork and self-discipline."

The soccer ball agreed, and it got quiet again. They both waited for the next day.

Classify

Sometimes when you read, you find groups that go together. For example, you can group shapes, colors, or animals.

1. Read the text. Then read the list below. Write each item in the correct column on the chart.

rain	iceberg	steam	water	hail
puddle	snowman	vapor	icicle	ocean

Solid	Liquid	Gas

2. Identify the state of matter for each thing listed below.

   _____ car exhaust fumes   _____ gasoline

   _____ lava   _____ ice cream

   _____ ink   _____ helium in a balloon

   _____ rock   _____ wood

Critical Thinking

How did classifying each example as a solid, a liquid, or a gas help you to understand what you read?

_____

_____

_____

STATES OF MATTER

There are three states of matter: solid, liquid, and gas. Matter can exist in any of these states. Let's use water as an example to think about these states.

Solid

When water is a solid, we call it ice. You can skate on it or put some of it into your glass to make your drink cold.

Liquid

When water is a liquid, you can swim in it, drink it, or take a shower with it. You can water plants or fill your fishbowl, too.

Gas

When water is a gas, it is called water vapor or steam. You can see steam as it rises from a boiling pot or a cup of hot coffee. Clouds are made of water vapor. When the water vapor condenses back into liquid droplets, it falls as rain.

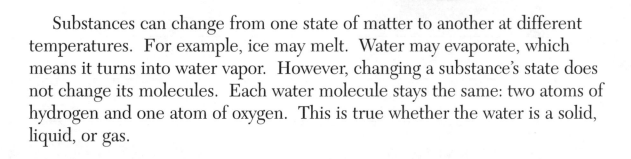

Substances can change from one state of matter to another at different temperatures. For example, ice may melt. Water may evaporate, which means it turns into water vapor. However, changing a substance's state does not change its molecules. Each water molecule stays the same: two atoms of hydrogen and one atom of oxygen. This is true whether the water is a solid, liquid, or gas.

Classify

Sometimes when you read, you find groups that go together. For example, you can group shapes, colors, or animals.

1. Read the text. Use the pictures at the bottom of the text to decide which are insects and which are not. Write each in the correct column below.

| butterfly | ladybug | tick | grasshopper |
| spider | worm | cockroach | centipede |

Insect	Not an Insect

Critical Thinking

How did identifying which of the animals are insects help you to understand what you read?

_____

_____

_____

What Makes an Insect an Insect?

How are an ant, a bee, and a fly all alike? That's right—they are all insects. But what makes them insects? For one thing, they all have six jointed legs. They also have three main body parts: a head, a thorax, and an abdomen.

An insect's head has eyes, a mouth, and two antennae. The antennae are used for smelling and tasting and can sense motion, heat, and sound. The middle part of an insect's body is the thorax. If an insect has wings, this is where they are located. The hind part of an insect's body is usually the largest. It is the insect's abdomen.

Insects have skeletons that are on the *outside* of their bodies. That's why they are called exoskeletons. These skeletons are very hard, and they protect the soft inside part of the insect's body.

Insects are the most diverse group of animals on Earth. There are more than a million known insect species. They represent more than half of all known living creatures. Scientists think there may be millions more to discover.

The next time you see a bug, look at it closely. Is it an insect or not?

butterfly

centipede

ladybug

tick

cockroach

spider

worm

grasshopper

Cause and Effect

A cause makes something else happen. The effect is what happens. When you read, notice cause-and-effect relationships. This will help you to understand how and why things occur.

1. Read the text. Explain what causes your stomach to contract.

   _____

2. Explain the effect (result) of having low glucose in your blood.

   _____

3. Write the missing cause or effect below.

Cause: _____
Effect: Your brain gets a message that you are hungry.
Cause: Your *appestat* feels that your stomach is full.
Effect: _____
Cause: _____
Effect: Your body has fuel to use.

Critical Thinking

What might happen to a person whose appestat does not work properly?

_____

_____

_____

Why You Feel Hungry

Have you ever wondered why you feel hungry? It's your stomach reminding you that it is time to eat. When your stomach is empty, it begins to *contract*. Contract means squeeze together. It does about three contractions per minute. If you don't eat, the contractions start happening more often. This is the way your stomach sends the message to your brain, "Hey! I need food. Hurry up!"

The part of your brain that gives you that empty feeling is called the *appestat*. It is also the appestat that tells you to stop eating when you are full. Scientists do not yet understand exactly how the appestat works. Some think it may work like the thermostat in your house. When your blood is low on a fuel called glucose, the appestat yells, "Time to eat!" When the glucose in your blood rises, the appestat says, "Stop eating now; you're full."

And here's surprising news: How you feel while you eat affects the food in your stomach! If you are feeling happy, the food gets digested quickly. Digestion turns food into fuel that your body can use. However, if you are feeling angry or sad, the food may just sit in your stomach and can even make you feel sick. Obviously, it is better to be a happy eater than an angry or sad eater!

Cause and Effect

A cause makes something else happen. The effect is what happens. When you read, notice cause-and-effect relationships. This will help you to understand how and why things occur.

1. Read the text. Explain what causes clouds to move across the sky.

   _____

2. Explain the effect (result) of the sun shining on Earth.

   _____

3. Write the missing cause or effect below.

Cause: _____
Effect: Clouds form.
Cause: Jet pilots felt their planes pulled along by jet streams.
Effect: _____
Cause: _____
Effect: These winds were named *jet streams*.

Critical Thinking

Why are the jet streams important to us?

_____

_____

_____

Jet Streams

Some days there are clouds in the sky, and some days there are not. Have you ever wondered why? Where do clouds come from? Where do they go? You might know part of the answer. Winds move clouds across the sky. You might not know why it happens. All weather takes place in the layer of air closest to Earth's surface. Many things affect weather, including heat, water, and wind.

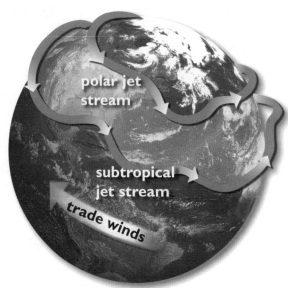

The sun shines on Earth's surface and makes it warmer. This causes heat and moisture to rise into the sky and form clouds. These clouds are pushed and pulled by winds high above the Earth called *jet streams*. Jet streams are like rivers of wind. They are thousands of miles long, hundreds of miles wide, and several miles deep. There are four main jet streams.

Jet streams change our weather. They blow the moisture around so more clouds form in one area than another. Their winds blow about 125 miles per hour (201 kph). However, unlike actual rivers, jet streams don't stay in the same place. They bend and move toward the equator, or they bend and move away from the equator.

Jet streams were discovered in modern times. After jet planes were invented, they flew high enough above Earth to enter the jet streams. The pilots felt their planes pulled along (or held back) by the jet stream's high winds.

Draw Conclusions

When you draw conclusions, you make decisions based on what you read. The information is not stated in the text. You must figure it out from the information provided. If you need to, reread the story to decide the answers.

1. Read the story. What can you tell about Marta's personality?

   _____

   _____

2. Do you think there are dragons in this forest? Explain.

   _____

   _____

3. Will Marta encounter a dragon? What made you draw this conclusion?

   _____

   _____

Critical Thinking

Is the village boy the only person who believes in the existence of dragons? Explain.

_____

_____

_____

Marta's Decision

Marta was afraid. The large, dark forest had many dangers lurking in it. There were sheer cliffs and spiky brambles. There were poisonous plants with leaves that could give you a painful rash. But, mostly there were the creatures. The normal animals were frightening enough. Snakes, spiders, wolves, and bears hid in the shadows. Any one of them could be deadly if forced to defend itself. However, what really worried Marta was that the forest was said to have dragons!

Now, ordinarily Marta was not the kind of girl to listen to rumors. However, the village boy had seemed so certain. He said that the dragons are enormous. The adult dragons are the size of a large barn. They have bright-colored scales that sparkle in the light. Yet they have the ability to blend into any landscape in an instant. Their huge heads hold razor-sharp teeth that drip with venom. Although their reptilian bodies are cool to the touch, hot breath curls around their faces like steam. Great wings fold tightly against their muscular backs. Anita, the old blind woman, swears that those wings can carry the beasts all the way to the sun.

Marta had to make a decision. She peered cautiously into the dimness between the trees. No one would blame her if she turned back. Yet her errand was important. She had to admit that as frightened as she felt, she was also curious. Was it really possible that dragons lived inside this little forest?

"Probably not," she thought, "but how amazing would it be if they did?" Quickly, before she could change her mind, she hurried toward the trees.

Draw Conclusions

When you draw conclusions, you make decisions based on what you read. The information is not stated in the text. You must figure it out from the information provided. If you need to, reread the story to decide the answers.

1. Read the text. Is it nonfiction or fiction? Explain.

   _____

   _____

2. Are Dorothy and her friends visitors to the Emerald City or are they returning home to the Emerald City? How do you know?

   _____

   _____

3. Draw a picture of the city based on the description given.

   [drawing box]

Critical Thinking

Do you think that Dorothy is fascinated with or frightened by the Emerald City? Explain.

_____

_____

_____

Dorothy and the Emerald City

Adapted from *The Wizard of Oz* by L. Frank Baum

Even with my eyes protected by my green glasses, my friends and I were dazzled by the wonderful city. The streets were lined with beautiful houses. Their windowpanes were of green glass. All were built of green marble and studded with sparkling emeralds. We walked over pavement made of the same green marble, and where the blocks joined together were rows of close-set emeralds. They glittered in the sun's light. Even the sky above the city had a green tint, and the rays of the sun were green!

There were many men, women, and children walking about. They were all dressed in green clothes and had greenish skin. Their wondering eyes followed me and my unusual company. The children all hid behind their mothers when they saw the lion. No one spoke to us.

Many shops stood in the street, and I saw that everything in them was green. I saw green candy and green popcorn, as well as green shoes, green hats, and green clothing. In one place, a man was selling green lemonade, and when the children bought it, I could see that they paid for it with green coins.

There seemed to be no horses or animals of any kind. The men carried things around in little green carts which they pushed before them. Everyone seemed happy.

Infer

When you infer, you make decisions based on information you read. The information is not given. You must figure it out from the information provided. If you need to, reread the story to decide the answers.

1. Read the text. What is the animal? How do you know?

_____

_____

2. Why are there so many different descriptions of the same animal?

_____

_____

3. How is the little girl wise?

_____

_____

_____

Critical Thinking

Could this story really have happened? Explain.

_____

_____

_____

What Animal Is This?

Outside a small village, an interesting animal was found that no one had ever seen before. The people wanted to know what it was and if it had any practical use. They took the animal to the six village elders. All six men were blind, but they were extremely wise.

The first wise man went up to the animal and touched its solid leg. He stated, "This animal is a strong pillar that could hold up a heavy roof."

The second wise man walked to the back of the animal and touched its tail. He exclaimed, "The animal is a rope. It could be used to tie things together."

Then the third wise man approached the animal and felt its big floppy ear. He said, "No, not a rope or a pillar. This animal is a fan that could be used to cool people on hot days."

The fourth wise man approached the side of the animal and touched its belly. He ran his hand up the animal's side and stretched his arm up as far as he could. Suddenly he declared, "This animal is a wall. It could be used to protect us against attacks from invaders."

The fifth wise man came up to the front of the animal and touched the end of its sharp tusk. He declared, "This animal is a spear. It could be used to hunt animals."

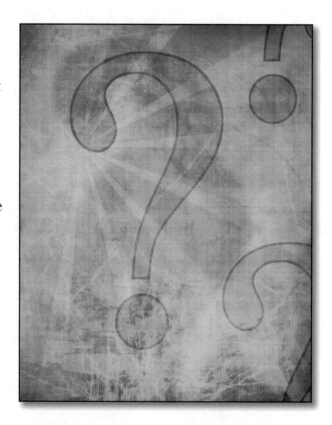

Finally, the sixth wise man went to the front of the animal. He touched its trunk and said, "You are all wrong! This animal is a long tube. It could be used like a hose to move water."

Then a little girl stepped forward and said, "Each of you is right, but all of you are wrong. You just need to listen to each other."

Infer

When you infer, you make decisions based on information you read. The information is not given. You must figure it out from the information provided. If you need to, reread the story to decide the answers.

1. Read the text. Why is it dangerous to have filthy hospitals?

   _____

   _____

2. Was Florence Nightingale a person who thought for herself? Explain.

   _____

   _____

3. Was Florence Nightingale a hard worker? Explain.

   _____

   _____

Critical Thinking

Why did people go to see Florence Nightingale instead of going to a doctor for advice about taking care of patients?

   _____

   _____

   _____

The Lady with the Lamp

Long ago, hospitals were different than they are today. Most were very dirty. They were full of diseases. Many patients died there. A woman named Florence Nightingale wanted to change that.

Florence Nightingale was born in 1820. She liked taking care of sick people and decided to become a nurse. She attended nursing school and was a very good student. However, back then, no one knew what caused disease or sickness. They had no idea that unclean conditions led to disease!

During a war, Florence ran a hospital for soldiers. It was a huge, dirty barracks. Many soldiers were dying there. Florence tried to keep them alive, but she was frustrated. She thought it might help more men to survive if they were kept in cleaner conditions. So, she cleaned the hospital each night. Since she carried a lamp to light her way as she worked, people called her "the lady with the lamp." Her action saved thousands of men's lives.

PRESENTED WITH "YULE TIDE," 1891.

THE LADY WITH THE LAMP.
(MISS NIGHTINGALE AT SCUTARI, 1854.)
FROM THE PAINTING BY HENRIETTA RAE (MRS. NORMAND).

Florence Nightingale became an expert in the care of sick and injured patients. People from around the world came to her for advice. She is the founder of modern nursing.

Summarize

A summary sentence tells what a paragraph is about. It may be at the start or the end of a paragraph. If there is no summary sentence, think how you could state the main idea in one sentence.

1. Read the text. Write the summary sentence from the first paragraph.

   _____

2. Write the summary sentence from the second paragraph.

   _____

3. Write the summary sentence from the third paragraph.

   _____

4. Write your own sentence that summarizes the whole text.

   _____

   _____

Critical Thinking

How do summary sentences help you to understand a text?

   _____

   _____

   _____

Hawaiian Quilts

Hawaiian quilts are unique. These quilts usually have two colors of cloth. One color is for the background. The other color is for the design.

These quilts are made with the snowflake method. This means that the design is cut all at once. Then, white thread is used to stitch the design to the background. (Long ago, this was the only thread people had.) These methods help to make the Hawaiian quilts look different from all other quilts.

Hawaiian quilts show the natural beauty of Hawaii. The patterns may use colorful flowers or the shapes of Hawaiian leaves and plants. Other quilts have animal designs. This makes Hawaiian quilts easy to recognize.

Summarize

A summary sentence tells what a paragraph is about. It may be at the start or the end of a paragraph. If there is no summary sentence, think how you could state the main idea in one sentence.

1. Read the text. Write a summary sentence for each paragraph.

   Paragraph 1: _____

   Paragraph 2: _____

   Paragraph 3: _____

   Paragraph 4: _____

   Paragraph 5: _____

2. Write two sentences of your own that summarize the whole text.

   _____

   _____

   _____

Critical Thinking

How does writing a summary of a text make you concentrate on its main idea?

_____

_____

_____

Chesapeake Bay

Chesapeake Bay is a beautiful place where the water meets the land. It is a large bay surrounded by Maryland, Virginia, and the Atlantic Ocean. People come from all over to sail, fish, and sightsee there. But Chesapeake Bay is more than a popular vacation spot.

Chesapeake Bay has some of the most famous coastal wetlands in the world. It has a long, ragged coast. Fingers of water push inland from the bay. They feed the wetlands and the animals and plants living there.

There are many plant and animal habitats in Chesapeake Bay. One of the largest habitats is the wetlands. In wetlands, plants and animals live both above and below the water. There are different kinds of wetlands. Some have mainly trees with a few bushes. Others have mainly grasses and bushes. Chesapeake Bay has both freshwater and tidal wetlands.

What makes an area a wetland? There are some key features. The first is, of course, the water. Wetlands have shallow water. The freshwater wetlands of the Chesapeake Bay are just a few feet deep. The tidal wetlands can be shallow or deep. It depends on the tides.

Wetlands provide a home for plants that are able to live in water and wet soils all the time. When the plants and trees die, they fall into the water and rot. Animals, bugs, and bacteria eat this rotting material.

Wetlands have running freshwater.

Chesapeake Bay coastline

An egret finds food in the shallow water.

Paraphrase

When you paraphrase, you restate the information in a text in your own words.

1. Read the text. Write one sentence to paraphrase each paragraph. In some cases, there is a topic sentence that does this for you.

_____

_____

_____

_____

2. Paraphrase the whole text in your own words in one or two sentences.

_____

_____

_____

_____

Critical Thinking

Think of a time when you had to paraphrase something. Briefly tell about it.

_____

_____

_____

Families Then and Now

Long ago, people lived and worked in cities, towns, and the country. Children studied, did a lot of chores, and played when they could. Families ate meals together and went to church together. They took care of each other.

Families back then were not much different from families today. They were the same in the most important ways, like caring for and loving each other. But they were different in some ways, too.

Long ago, everyone in the family worked.

Long ago, adults worked hard all day long. Most men were farmers. They took care of crops and animals, did repairs, and provided food for their families. The women cared for the homes and the children. They prepared food, cleaned, spun thread, and sewed clothes. Often, children had to work alongside their parents to get everything done.

Today, families also work but have more free time to spend with each other.

Adults today work hard, too, but they usually don't work as many hours. They have more time off. Stores and inventions have made life easier. For example, most people buy food and clothing from stores instead of making their own. Most children do not have to work to help keep the family going. Some adults work away from home and spend the rest of the time with their families. Others work at home and take care of their families at the same time.

Paraphrase

When you paraphrase, you restate the information in a text in your own words.

1. Read the text. Write one sentence to paraphrase each paragraph. In three of the paragraphs, there is a topic sentence that does this for you.

   _____

   _____

   _____

   _____

2. What is another word for *jester*?

   _____

3. Explain the one function of a modern clown working in a rodeo.

   _____

   _____

Critical Thinking

How did summing up the text in your own words help you to understand what you read?

_____

_____

_____

Jesters of Old, Clowns of Today

When we hear the word *clown*, we usually think of the circus. But clowns were around long before they became a part of the circus. The first clowns were called *jesters*. They were the "fools" in the royal courts during the Middle Ages. They had the job of amusing the king and his family. Jesters dressed in costumes. They wore caps and pointed shoes with bells. As they performed for the king, the bells moved and jingled. Jesters were often very close to the royalty they served. They played with the children and took part in family events. Not only were they funny, but they were often very clever. Some may have even given advice to the leaders they served.

In the early American circus, clowns were like comedians. They sang, danced, and told jokes in a single ring. When the circus grew to include three rings, clowns started to do *pantomime*. This is when they perform their acts without using any words.

Today, clowns perform at the circus and the rodeo. At the circus, they provide comic relief. Usually they do this between tension-filled acts by other performers. Some clowns also perform funny versions of circus acts. They are usually very good at them, too. They do things like walk the tightrope, perform tricks in the air, and ride horses bareback. At the rodeo, clowns amuse the audience. They may also be used to distract dangerous animals. While they do this, injured performers are rescued from the arena.

Each clown's costume and makeup are unique. In fact, one clown cannot wear his or her makeup in exactly the same way as any other clown. Most clowns are in *whiteface*. This means that they apply white grease paint all over their faces. Then they use other colors to create mouths and eyes. Noses are made from a special kind of putty.

Table of Contents

A table of contents appears at the start of a nonfiction book. It tells the chapters that are in the book. By scanning the table of contents, you can tell if the book might answer a question you have.

1. Scan the table of contents. What is the name of the third chapter?

   _____

2. Look at the chapter title on page 3. Predict what you would read about in that chapter.

   _____

   _____

3. Read the table of contents. How many chapters are there in this book? (Note: the glossary and the index are not chapters.) _____

4. If you turn to page 21, what will you read about?

   _____

5. On which page does the information about the stomach begin? _____

Critical Thinking

How does a book's table of contents differ from its index?

_____

_____

_____

The Digestive System

Table of Contents

Table of Contents

A table of contents appears at the start of a nonfiction book. It tells the chapters that are in the book. By scanning the table of contents, you can tell if the book might answer a question you have.

1. Scan the table of contents on the next page. What is the name of the sixth chapter? (Hint: only chapters have page numbers.)

   _____

2. Look at the chapter title for page 78. Predict what you would read about.

   _____

   _____

3. Read the table of contents. How many chapters are there in this book? (Note: The glossary and the index are not chapters.) _____

4. If you turn to page 102, what will you read about?

   _____

5. On which page does the information about Northeastern tribes begin?

   _____

Critical Thinking

When would you use a table of contents?

_____

_____

_____

American Indians

Table of Contents

Index

An index is always on the last pages of a nonfiction book. It is a list of important topics that are covered in the book. Specific words and ideas are given their own listings. If you want to see if a word is mentioned in a book, use the index.

1. Scan the index. How are the entries listed—in the order in which they appear in the book or alphabetically? How do you know?

   _____

   _____

2. On what pages would you find information about *larvae*?

   _____

3. If you turned to page 22, what would you read about?

   _____

4. If you wanted to learn about *mollusks*, what is the first page you would turn to?

   _____

Critical Thinking

Why isn't there an index in the back of a fiction book?

_____

_____

_____

Invertebrates

Index

An index is always on the last pages of a nonfiction book. It is a list of important topics that are covered in the book. Specific words and ideas are given their own listings. If you want to see if a word is mentioned in a book, use the index.

1. Scan the index. The book is about Roberto Clemente. How many other Clementes are mentioned?

   _____

2. What can you predict about Robert Clemente from this index?

   _____

3. Read the index. If you turn to pages 3–11 what will you read about?

   _____

4. If you want to read about Robert Clemente's being named Most Valuable Player, what is the first page you would turn to?

   _____

Critical Thinking

How does a book's index differ from its table of contents?

_____

_____

_____

Roberto Clemente

Glossary

A glossary is like a very short dictionary placed in the back of a nonfiction book. The glossary lists the definitions of important words used in the book. If you are reading and don't understand a word, turn to the glossary.

1. Scan the glossary. You will see some words that you don't know. List two below.

    _____   _____

2. Read the text. Write the definition of one word that you listed above.

    _____

3. Use the word *Braille* in a sentence.

    _____

    _____

4. Use the word *email* in a sentence.

    _____

    _____

Critical Thinking

When would you use a glossary?

_____

_____

_____

Inventions in Communication

Glossary

antenna—a wire that receives or transmits radio and TV signals

Braille—a system of raised dots which allows the blind to read

broadcast—to send out radio or TV signals

cell phone—a portable phone that works by radio waves

cell tower—a tower with many antennas that transmit and receive radio waves from cell phones

email—an electronic message sent between linked computers

fiber optic cable—a bundle of thin glass fibers that carry information in the form of light energy

hieroglyphics—a form of writing made of pictures and symbols used by ancient Egyptians

instant messaging—keying messages over the Internet in real time

Internet—a worldwide system of linked computer networks

manual alphabet—a method of spelling words using the fingers

network—a group of things connected to each other

online—connected to the Internet

satellite—an object that orbits Earth

scroll—a piece of parchment with writing on it that rolls up into the shape of a tube

search engine—software that scans the World Wide Web for requested information

switchboard—the control panel for connecting the lines of a telephone system

typewriter—a machine that prints letters, numbers, and punctuation marks on paper when you press keys with your fingers

website—a group of linked pages that can be viewed online

word processor—a machine or computer program used to type, edit, store, and print documents

Glossary

A glossary is like a very short dictionary placed in the back of a nonfiction book. The glossary lists the definitions of important words used in the book. If you are reading and don't understand a word, turn to the glossary.

1. Scan the glossary. You will see some words you don't know. List two below.

    _____   _____

2. Read the text. Write the definition of one word that you listed above.

    _____

    _____

3. Use the word *famine* in a sentence.

    _____

    _____

4. Some of the words in this glossary have information in parentheses that immediately follows the term. What is this information?

    _____

    _____

Critical Thinking

How does a glossary differ from an index?

_____

_____

_____

Immigration

Glossary

ancestor—someone who comes earlier in a family, such as a
    great-grandmother

assimilation (uh-SIM-uh-LAY-shun)—absorbed and incorporated (added
    to)

detained—held for questioning

diplomat—a person representing his or her nation's government in a
    foreign country

emigrate—to leave a place of residence to in another place

ethnicity (eth-NISS-it-ee)—a particular ethnic (cultural) group

excluded—refused entrance to the nation

exploited—treated poorly

famine (FAM-uhn)—an extreme lack of food

harassed—tormented, mistreated

immigrant—a person who moves permanently to a new nation

influx—the arrival of large numbers of people

interpreter—a person who understands more than one language and
    assists the communication between people who cannot speak the
    same language

meager (MEE-gur)—barely enough

migration—the movement of people from one region or nation to
    another

pauper—a person who has no money and no means of support except for
    charity

piecework—wages earned based on the number of pieces completed

quota—a fixed number

restriction (ri-STRIK-shun)—a limitation

swindler—a person who cheats another out of money or property

tenement—a run-down apartment building in a poor section of a city

Answer Key

Preview, p. 8

1. Answers will vary; students may know that there are ingredients and step-by-step directions on any recipe.
2. Answers will vary. Sample: There are measurements for the ingredients and step-by-step directions.
3. Answers will vary. Samples: Yes, in most recipes, you have to cook or bake the item. OR I've never heard of sprinkling nutmeg on top of a drink before.

Critical Thinking answers will vary. Samples: It would be wise to preview a recipe to be sure you like all of the ingredients; to be sure you have all the ingredients you will need; to be sure that you have the materials (measuring tools, blender, etc.) you will need.

Preview, p. 10

1. Answers will vary. Sample: I think that this text will be about how skateboards have evolved over the years.
2. Answers will vary. Samples:
   1900s: The first skateboard had a handle and a crate.
   1950s: The crate and handles were removed.
   1959: Skateboards were sold in stores.
   1965: Skateboards were so dangerous that the sport almost died completely.
   1975: Urethane wheels and a kick tail made more tricks possible and revived the sport.

Critical Thinking answers will vary. Sample: Previewing helped me to understand because I knew what the topic was, so I could think about what I already knew about skateboarding.

Predict, p. 12

1. Answers will vary. Sample: I think this story will be about a black horse.
2. Answers will vary. Sample: The mother will tell Black Beauty to be kind to friends.
3. Answers will vary. Sample: Black Beauty's mother wants him to be a gentle, respectful horse.
4. Answers will vary. Sample: I predict that since Black Beauty never forgot his mother's advice that he will behave in a gentle manner at all times.

Critical Thinking answers will vary. Sample: I did not think that the story would be told by a horse.

Predict, p. 14

1.–2. Your Prediction: Answers will vary. What Actually Happened: Emily was separated from the wagon train when she ran into the woods; Emily cannot find her way back to the wagon train; Emily is found by the adults from the wagon train.

Critical Thinking answers will vary. Sample: Making predictions helps me think about what might logically happen next.

Prior Knowledge, p. 16

1. Answers will vary. Sample: I know that crayons come in many colors and that they are made of wax.
2. Pictures will vary but should show a crayon mold.
3. Answers will vary. Sample: No, because blue is one of my favorite colors, too.

Critical Thinking answers will vary. Sample: Reading this text would be more difficult if I had never used a crayon because I would be unfamiliar with them. As it is, I can picture crayons in my mind and know what it's like to color with them and can recall the way they smell.

Answer Key *(cont.)*

Prior Knowledge, p. 18

1. Answers will vary, but most students of this age have already been involved in a fundraising activity at school, church, or some other organization (such as Boy Scouts).
2. Answers will vary. Sample: I know that most metal cans and plastic bottles are recyclable.
3. Answers will vary. Sample: Jen and her dance team will collect bottles and take them to a recycling center to redeem them for money.

Critical Thinking answers will vary. Sample: Because I already know about how hard it is to fundraise and about recycling bottles for money, I was able to appreciate what a clever idea Jen had.

Set a Purpose, p. 20

1. Answers will vary. Sample: How high can dolphins jump?
2. Answers will vary; accept any two facts from the text. Sample: Dolphins use sounds to find things; Dolphins have been known to rescue people.
3. Answers will vary. Sample: I wish the fifth paragraph had more information because I want to know more about how dolphins help people who are drowning.

Critical Thinking answers will vary. Sample: No, my question was not answered. I can look up the answer online, in an encyclopedia, or in a library book.

Set a Purpose, p. 22

1. Answers will vary. Sample: How can a person be a careful shopper?
2. Answers will vary. Sample: This text will be about a grocery store or grocery shopping. I know because the photo shows a grocery cart.
3. Answers will vary. Samples: Companies try to make their food seem tasty in TV commercials; Companies pay to have their products placed on the shelves at eye level.

Critical Thinking answers will vary. Sample: No, but I can look up the answer online, in an encyclopedia, or in a library book.

Ask Questions, p. 24

1. Answers will vary. Sample: I predict that the story will be about a gorilla.
2. Answers will vary. Sample: I think the inflatable gorilla was stolen.
3. Answers will vary; accept any two facts: Someone stole the inflatable gorilla from on top of a car dealership; No one saw who did it; The gorilla turned up on the football field at Maple Hills High school; Maple Hills is playing Lincoln High in the big game tonight; The dealership's owner says that Maple Hills can keep it until the game is over; The owner graduated from Maple Hills.
4. Answers will vary. Sample: How much does the inflatable gorilla weigh?

Critical Thinking answers will vary. Sample: I like the question-and-answer format because it is like listening in on a conversation.

Ask Questions, p. 26

1.–3. Answers will vary. Samples: What I Know: A Tasmanian Devil is an animal; What I Want to Know: Is it like a bear or a squirrel?; What I Learned: This animal is the size of a large dog and looks like a bear cub.

Critical Thinking answers will vary. Sample: I can look it up online, in an encyclopedia, or in a library book.

Make Connections, p. 28

1. Answers will vary. Sample: My family wanted to go to the beach, but I wanted to stay home and play with my friends.
2. Answers will vary. Sample: I was glad to meet my friend Keisha when I started at my new school.
3. Answers will vary. Sample: I'm like Luke because I'm not shy.
4. Answers will vary. Sample: Yes, because a ship has a lot of fun things to do.

Critical Thinking answers will vary. Sample: Making connections to my own life helps me to understand how Abby feels at the start of the vacation.

Answer Key *(cont.)*

Make Connections, p. 30

1. Answers will vary. Sample: I would like to go camping because I like being outdoors and sleeping in a tent.
2. Answers will vary. Sample: David chose Evan to camp with him because Jack, his best friend, probably wouldn't enjoy camping and Evan would like it.
3. Answers will vary. Sample: David could have asked Jack if he'd like to try camping.

Critical Thinking answers will vary. Sample: I think it was a good choice because David can build his friendship with Evan.

Context Clues, p. 32

1. *igloo, insulator, construct*
2. Answers will vary. Sample: An *igloo* is a round, temporary home made from snow blocks. I know because it is described in the text and there is a photo of one.
3. Answers will vary. Sample: The word *insulator* means something that keeps the cold air out and keeps the warm air in. I know because that's how the snow is described in the text.
4. Answers will vary. Sample: The word *construct* means to build. I know because the word "build" can be substituted for the word "construct" in the sentence in the text.

Critical Thinking answers will vary. Sample: The text described what is inside an igloo.

Context Clues, p. 34

1. Answers will vary. Sample: The word *distressed* means upset. The clue is that Ms. Jackson broke down and wept because she lost her dog.
2. Answers will vary. Sample: The word *eavesdrop* means to listen without anyone knowing. The clue is that Katrina tiptoed closer and had to strain to hear.
3. Answers will vary. Sample: The word *dawned* means realized. The clue is that Katrina starts to realize what the women are talking about.

Critical Thinking answers will vary. Sample: Using context helps me understand more difficult texts because I can use the sentences and words to figure out what unknown words mean.

Visualize, p. 36

1. Picture must show a solid green flag.
2. Student must draw the French flag.
3. Student must draw the Japanese flag.

Critical Thinking answers will vary. Sample: Making pictures in my mind let me "see" the flags of the nations that are described but not shown in the illustrations.

Visualize, p. 38

1. Drawings will vary but should show a shepherd putting sheep into a stable.
2. Drawings will vary but should show a shepherd feeding wild sheep more than his own sheep.
3. Drawings will vary but should show the wild sheep running away, the shepherd yelling at the sheep at the base of a mountain, or one sheep talking to the shepherd.

Critical Thinking answers will vary. Sample: It was like making a movie in my mind, so I saw the story unfold as it happens.

Story Elements, p. 40

1. Maria, Ariel, Mrs. Alvarez
2. Answers will vary. Sample: The story takes place along a road, probably in recent times because there is a car.
3. Answers will vary. Sample: The conflict is that the girls are out in the open as a tornado is coming.
4. Answers will vary. Sample: The conflict is solved when Mrs. Alvarez finds them, the girls get in the car and outrun the tornado, and they all get into a storm cellar.

Critical Thinking answers will vary. Samples: They will go outside and find that their car has been destroyed; They will go and search for their bikes on the road.

Answer Key *(cont.)*

Story Elements, p. 42

1. Javier
2. The story takes place in the present on a baseball field.
3. Answers will vary. Sample: The conflict is that Javier is not a good batter and yet his team is depending on him to hit the ball.
4. Answers will vary. Sample: Javier surprises everyone and hits a home run.

Critical Thinking answers will vary. Samples: Yes, Javier will gain confidence from this home run and become the best batter on his baseball team. OR No, Javier is still the worst hitter on the team, but maybe he'll get better with more practice.

Plot, p. 44

1. Sarah and Ming are best friends.
2. Answers will vary. Sample: Ming is upset because Sarah borrows Ming's special pencil and then loses it.
3. Answers will vary. Sample: Sarah ignores Ming the next day.
4. Answers will vary. Sample: Ming's father suggests that Ming should not be angry because a friend is more important than a pencil.

Critical Thinking answers will vary. Samples: I think that Sarah will not forgive Ming. OR As soon as Ming asks Sarah to forgive her, they will be friends again.

Plot, p. 46

1. Answers will vary. Sample: Brandon is worried because he wants to make the baseball team.
2. Answers will vary. Sample: Brandon makes a wish on a star because he hopes it will help him to make the baseball team.
3. Answers will vary. Sample: At the baseball tryouts, Brandon hits the ball over the fence.
4. Answers will vary. Sample: Brandon's problem is resolved because the story implies that he makes the team.

Critical Thinking answers will vary. Sample: It is very important for a story's problem to have a solution so that a reader finds out what happens.

Characters, p. 48

1. Mrs. Gerson, Juan, Nick, Ty, Lee, Andy
2. Answers will vary. Sample: Mrs. Gerson is old, but she is determined to hit a home run.
3. Answers will vary. Sample: The boys are trying to let Mrs. Gerson get a home run, so they don't throw the ball where it's supposed to go.
4. Answers will vary. Sample: The team members learned that Mrs. Gerson still enjoys having fun.

Critical Thinking answers will vary. Sample: Mrs. Gerson reminds me of my grandmother because she likes to play soccer with me.

Characters, p. 50

1. Answers will vary. Samples: Woodpecker's Actions: kind, helpful; Woodpecker's Words: "I will see what I can do for you." Lion's Actions: rude, selfish; Lion's Words: "I have already done a great deal for you. You cannot expect me to do anything more for you."
2. Answers will vary. Sample: The woodpecker learned that she should stay away from the lion because he is rude and selfish.

Critical Thinking answers will vary. Sample: I would rather have the Woodpecker as a friend because she would help me when I needed it.

Title and Headings, p. 52

1. Answers will vary. Sample: Taste: Our tongues can taste sweet and salty foods; Smell: Our noses help us to taste foods; Touch: Our sense of touch affects how we taste foods.
2. Answers will vary. Sample: The headings divide the text into sections that make it easier for me to find information.

Critical Thinking answers will vary. Sample: The headings make this text easier to understand because they make it clear that each sense affects the flavors of foods.

Answer Key (cont.)

Title and Headings, p. 54

1. Answers will vary. Sample: I think that the text will be about African art, especially textiles and jewelry.
2. Heading: African Textiles; accept any two facts from the text; Heading: African Jewelry; accept any two facts from the text

Critical Thinking answers will vary. Sample: The writer uses headings to divide this text into sections to show the two different types of art.

Typeface and Captions, p. 56

1. I see normal, boldface, and italic typeface.
2. summited, erosion
3. Answers will vary. Sample: These definitions are included so that the reader can understand what the words mean.
4. Answers will vary. Sample: The caption helps me to see that most of Mauna Kea is beneath sea level while most of Mount Everest is above sea level.

Critical Thinking answers will vary. Samples: Comparison of World's Tallest Mountains; World's Tallest Mountains on Land and Sea.

Typeface and Captions, p. 58

1. italics
2. Irish Wolfhound, English Mastiff, Pekingese, Chihuahua, Yorkshire Terrier
3. Answers will vary. Sample: The italicized words are the actual names of dog breeds. They are set in a special typeface to make them stand out.
4. Answers will vary. Sample: The captions let me know what kind of dog is in the photo.

Critical Thinking answers will vary. Sample: I have seen Yorkshire Terriers and Chihuahuas.

Graphics, p. 60

1. Answers will vary. Sample: The top illustration shows a side view of the human eye.
2. Answers will vary. Sample: The bottom illustration shows how an image enters the eye and appears upside down on the retina.
3. Answers will vary. Sample: It was put in a sidebar because it is so strange that the writer felt it should be illustrated.

Critical Thinking answers will vary. Sample: No, it would have been too hard to draw a diagram of the eye without seeing how the parts look.

Graphics, p. 62

1. Answers will vary. Sample: The diagram shows how water moves through the environment.
2. Answers will vary. Sample: The text explains why the water falls on one side of a mountain range and not the other.
3. Answers will vary. Sample: The water in lakes and oceans evaporates into the sky; Water moves from a lake to the ocean by flowing down a river; Evaporated water rises into the sky and forms clouds.

Critical Thinking answers will vary. Sample: The diagram shows why a desert lies on one side of a mountain range.

Topic Sentences, p. 64

1. Saturn, the sixth planet from the sun, is the second largest planet in our solar system.
2. Saturn does not have a solid surface.
3. Saturn is the least round of all the planets.
4. Perhaps the most amazing thing about Saturn is the rings that surround it.

Critical Thinking answers will vary. Sample: The topic sentences are like the main idea of each paragraph, so if I write each one, I will have a summary of the text.

Answer Key *(cont.)*

Topic Sentences, p. 66

1. Pirates went by different names.
2. Since it was thought to be unlucky to have a woman aboard a ship, there were few female pirates.
3. Answers will vary. Sample: The topic sentences tell me what each paragraph is about. Then the paragraph describes the topic sentence in more detail.

Critical Thinking answers will vary. Sample: The next time I read a nonfiction text, I will look for topic sentences to guide me through the text.

Main Idea, p. 68

1. Answers will vary. Sample: The overall main idea is that highly trained guide dogs help disabled people do everyday things.
2. The six most important sentences from the text: Because guide dogs are so well trained, they are welcome everywhere; People who are blind may use guide dogs called seeing-eye dogs; Some people who have hearing problems have hearing-ear dogs; Volunteers spend months training each guide dog; Always ask the owner's permission before interacting with the dog, and don't be upset if the person says no; You should never give the guide dog commands.

Critical Thinking answers will vary. Sample: Finding the main idea of each paragraph helps me to summarize the text and understand the overall main idea.

Main Idea, p. 70

1. Main Idea: Genevieve and Joshua have invented a machine to teleport objects.
2. Answers will vary. Sample: Details: Genevieve and Joshua are testing the machine they created; They try to teleport a box of Chocolate Chip Munchies cookies; The box vanishes but does not reappear; Genevieve remembers to do the final step, and the box reappears; To celebrate, she eats a cookie and offers one to Joshua, too.

Critical Thinking answers will vary. Sample: It is more challenging to find the main idea in fiction because it isn't always stated in one sentence.

Details, p. 72

1. Answers will vary. Sample: Main Idea: Mario and Leah go through a lot of effort to see a beautiful place inside a cave.
2. Answers will vary. Sample: Details: Leah and Mario get dirty and tired as they crawl down a tunnel; They find a beautiful place with a chimney-like opening that lets in light from the moon and stars; Embedded in the cave walls are crystals that glow; Columns of colorful rock reach from the floor to the ceiling; It looks like a magical fairyland.

Critical Thinking answers will vary. Sample: I think it is easier to find the main idea and details in nonfiction because the main idea is usually stated clearly.

Details, p. 74

1. Answers will vary. Sample: Main Idea: Animals communicate in a wide variety of ways.
2. Answers will vary. Samples: Details: Dogs, cats, gorillas, beavers, and grasshoppers use sound to communicate; Black bears, deer, and foxes mark trees and bushes; Honeybees, electric eels, lightning bugs, and dogs show their intentions by their actions (dancing, body postures); Female animals and skunks give off scents; Wolves in a pack wrestle to determine rank.

Critical Thinking answers will vary. Sample: The details in fiction are not necessarily true. Fiction may be about things that are not real—like talking animals and science fiction. The details in nonfiction text are facts that can be proven true.

Answer Key (cont.)

Main Idea and Details, p. 76

1.–2. Answers will vary. Samples:

Main Idea
Paragraph 1: Isaac Newton is the scientist who stated the Laws of Motion.
Paragraph 2: Newton's First Law of Motion concerns inertia.
Paragraph 3: Newton's Second Law of Motion concerns acceleration.
Paragraph 4: Newton's Third Law of Motion describes action and reaction.

Detail
Three laws about objects and the forces that act upon them.
Inertia resists any change in motion (which includes being still). An object will remain still or stay moving in the same direction at constant speed until a force acts upon it. Friction is a force that slows things down.
An object will move in the same direction as the force that acts upon it. A stronger force is needed to make a heavier object accelerate at the same speed as a lightweight object.
For every action there is an equal and opposite reaction. A chair's weight pushes down on the floor and the floor pushes back on the chair .

Critical Thinking answers will vary. Sample: I looked for the details that best supported the main idea.

Chronological Order, p. 78

1. 5, 2, 4, 3, 1
2. 1518 B.C.: Thutmose I became the pharaoh; 1504 B.C.: Thutmose III became the pharaoh; 1497 B.C.: Hatshepsut made herself pharaoh; 1458 B.C.: Hatshepsut died.

Critical Thinking answers will vary. Sample: Authors write events in chronological order because it makes the most sense to tell a story from beginning to end.

Chronological Order, p. 80

1. 2, 3, 1, 5, 4
2. Answers will vary. Sample: It is helpful to have this text written in chronological order because it is easier to understand the process of creating a pearl necklace.

Critical Thinking answers will vary. Sample: I think that the process is the same, but the type of oyster used to make the pearl is different.

Logical Order, p. 82

1. one
2. one
3. two
4. After step 3, you must wait overnight for the glue to dry.
5. If the kit is missing any of its parts, you should call a toll-free number to get the part.

Critical Thinking answers will vary. Sample: The best time to stain or paint the birdhouse would be either after step 4 (best choice) or before step 1.

Logical Order, p. 84

1. first, next, then, finally
2. Answers will vary. Sample: 1. Write what you earn and what you spend; 2. Decide what you want to save for; 3. Make a list of total income; 4. Make a list of total expenses; 5. Subtract expenses from income to see if you'll have any money for savings.
3. Answers will vary. Sample: If Sari earns less than she wants to spend, then she will not be able to buy everything she wants or she will have to use her savings to buy what she wants.

Critical Thinking answers will vary. Sample: Sari might keep her money in a piggy bank or a savings account.

Fact and Opinion, p. 86

1. Answers will vary; accept any fact given by Mr. Skippy. Sample: His company wants the students' feedback.
2. Answers will vary; accept any opinion given by Shay. Sample: She thinks Pig Planet Nine is the best game ever.
3. O, F, F, F, O

Critical Thinking answers will vary. Sample: No, I would not like to play Pig Planet Nine because I like more realistic games.

Answer Key (cont.)

Fact and Opinion, p. 88

1. Answers will vary; accept any fact from the first paragraph. Sample: Brian and Tabitha liked the same favorite food.
2. Kobe Bryant is the best basketball player who has ever lived.
3. F, F, O, O, F

Critical Thinking answers will vary. Sample: My brother likes Mexican food the best, but I like Italian food the best. After arguing, we both agree that we each have our own opinions.

Proposition and Support, p. 90

1. Answers will vary. Sample: I think that the writer's proposition will be that all schools should be year-round.
2. Answers will vary. Sample: The traditional school year calendar was created when students needed to be home in the summer to help on the farm.
3. Answers will vary; accept any three of the following: Students must review everything they've forgotten after the long summer vacation; Students must readjust to going to school after two months of free time; Students will still have a month in the summer to go to summer camp or have a family vacation; School vacations will be spread out throughout the year, resulting in less student and teacher burn out.

Critical Thinking answers will vary. Sample: Some families may have a hard time going on vacation because it might be difficult to get the parents' and the kids' vacation times aligned.

Proposition and Support, p. 92

1.

Position 1: T. rex was a scavenger.
Support: T. rex had tiny arms that would not have been helpful in hunting. It may have been too heavy to run very fast. Its legs were built for walking long distances, like scavengers do. The part of T. rex's brain that picked up scent was especially large, which is important for a scavenger.

Position 2: T. rex was a predator.
Support: T. rex's bones were thick and heavy, which might mean that it could move fast to capture prey. Its small arms would not have been needed to catch food. Dinosaur bones have been found with what looks like T. rex tooth marks on them.

2. Answers will vary. Sample: I think that T. rex being a scavenger has more support because four facts are listed to support this idea.

Critical Thinking answers will vary. Sample: Proposition and support makes a statement and then gives reasons why the reader should believe it. It is like problem and solution because it identifies a problem and gives the solution.

Author's Purpose, p. 94

1. Answers will vary. Sample: The author wrote this text to tell people about an upcoming play on campus.
2. What: A play entitled *A Husband for Mama* will be performed; When: 2 p.m. this Friday; Where: in the school auditorium
3. Answers will vary. Sample: The author hopes the reader will come to see the play.

Critical Thinking answers will vary. Sample: This text reminds me of a movie preview or an advertisement because it's trying to get me to see the performance.

Answer Key (cont.)

Author's Purpose, p. 96

1. Answers will vary. Sample: The author wrote this text to encourage the reader to donate things to charity.

2. Answers will vary. Sample: The author feels that it is important to donate things to charity. I know because the text tells about how the donations will benefit the needy.

3. Answers will vary. Sample: The kids feel good about helping others.

Critical Thinking answers will vary. Sample: Yes, I would like to shop at a thrift store because I may find interesting things there. OR No, I only like new clothes and belongings, so I wouldn't shop at a thrift store.

Compare and Contrast, p. 98

1.

Baseball
uses a smaller, harder ball
game has nine innings
uses a bat, a ball, bases, and gloves
overhand pitches
has a larger playing field
Softball
uses a larger, softer ball
game has seven innings
uses a bat, a ball, bases, and gloves
underhand pitches
has a smaller playing field
Slow-pitch Softball
the ball is thrown slowly
ten players on a team
Fast-pitch Softball
the ball is thrown fast
nine players on a team

2. Answers will vary. Sample: I prefer to play baseball because I like to throw overhand not underhand.

Critical Thinking answers will vary. Sample: Baseball and softball are more alike because they use the same rules about strikes, outs, and how to run the bases.

Compare and Contrast, p. 100

1. Answers will vary. Sample:

soccer
• played on an outdoor field
• score by making goals
• players use their feet to kick the ball
• players use their heads to butt the ball
• eleven players on a team
both
• played around the world
• played in the Olympics
• balls are round and full of air
• played by two teams
• develop a player's mind and body
• players learn teamwork and self-discipline
basketball
• played on a court
• score by making baskets
• five players on a team
• players bounce, pass, and shoot the ball with their hands

2. Answers will vary. Sample: I would rather play soccer because I enjoy playing sports on grass.

Critical Thinking answers will vary. Student must state which sport he or she thinks is the most popular in this nation and give a reason why. Sample: I think that baseball is the most popular sport in America because almost everyone I know watches the World Series.

Classify, p. 102

1.

Solid	Liquid	Gas
• iceberg	• rain	• steam
• hail	• puddle	• vapor
• snowman	• water	
• icicle	• ocean	

2. gas: car exhaust fumes; liquid: gasoline; liquid: lava; solid: ice cream; liquid: ink; gas: helium in a balloon; solid: rock; solid: wood

Critical Thinking answers will vary. Sample: Classifying each example made me think about what I had read and about the states of matter of different things.

Answer Key (cont.)

Classify, p. 104

1.

Insect	Not an Insect
• butterfly	• spider
• ladybug	• worm
• cockroach	• centipede
• grasshopper	
• tick	

Critical Thinking answers will vary. Sample: Identifying the insects made me reread so I could be sure about the parts that insects have.

Cause and Effect, p. 106

1. Answers will vary. Sample: When your stomach is empty, it starts to contract.
2. Answers will vary. Sample: Low glucose in your blood causes the appestat to tell you that you are hungry and need to eat.
3. Cause: Your stomach starts to contract. Effect: Your brain gets the message that you are hungry. Cause: Your *appestat* feels that your stomach is full. Effect: You stop eating. Cause: Your body digests the food you ate. Effect: Your body has fuel to use.

Critical Thinking answers will vary, but students must state that a person whose appestat does not work properly might either overeat (because the appestat doesn't tell the person when he or she is full) or not eat enough (because the appestat doesn't tell the person when he or she is hungry).

Cause and Effect, p. 108

1. Answers will vary. Samples: Jet streams pull and push clouds across the sky. OR Winds cause the clouds to move across the sky.
2. Answers will vary. Sample: The sun heats the earth's surface and makes moisture rise into the sky to form clouds.
3. Cause: The sun causes heat and moisture to rise into the sky. Effect: Clouds form. Cause: Jet pilots felt their planes pulled along by jet streams. Effect: The pilots discovered the jet streams. Cause: Jet pilots discovered the rivers of wind high in the sky. Effect: These winds were named *jet streams*.

Critical Thinking answers will vary. Sample: Jet streams are important because they change our weather.

Draw Conclusions, p. 110

1. Answers will vary. Sample: Marta is responsible because she completes her errand even though she must pass through the scary forest.
2. Answers will vary. Sample: Yes, there are dragons in the forest; this story is a fantasy adventure and the dragons are what make it interesting.
3. Answers will vary. Samples: Yes, Marta will encounter a dragon. I think so because the story tells about other people who encountered dragons. OR No, Marta will not encounter a dragon on this trip through the forest but might when she thinks the forest is perfectly safe.

Critical Thinking answers will vary. Sample: No, the old blind woman seems to believe in the dragons, too. Also, Marta seems to believe they might exist.

Draw Conclusions, p. 112

1. This story is fiction. Explanations will vary. Sample: People do not have green skin and the sky is not green.
2. Dorothy and her friends are visitors to the Emerald City. Explanations will vary. Sample: I know because they are "dazzled by the wonderful city."
3. Drawings will vary but must be based on information from the text. It is important that everything in the drawing is some shade of green.

Critical Thinking answers will vary. Sample: Dorothy is fascinated with the Emerald City. She does not say anything in her description that makes me believe she is afraid.

Infer, p. 114

1. The animal is an elephant. Explanations will vary. Sample: I know because of the description of its body parts, especially its trunk and tusk.
2. Answers will vary. Sample: Each blind man only touched one part of the animal. The men didn't realize that the animal has a lot of different body parts.
3. Answers will vary. Sample: The girl is wise because she tells the men that each one is right about a body part but that they can only figure out what the animal is if they listen to each other and put all their ideas together.

Critical Thinking answers will vary. Sample: No, because someone would have probably explained to the men that they needed to feel the whole creature and not just one part of it.

Answer Key (cont.)

Infer, p. 116

1. Answers will vary. Sample: It is dangerous to have filthy hospitals because germs are everywhere. These germs can infect the patients and cause many to die.
2. Answers will vary. Sample: Yes, she decided that cleaner conditions might lead to fewer deaths, and then she took action.
3. Answers will vary. Sample: Yes, Florence Nightingale was a hard worker. Nobody told her to clean the hospital each night. She did so because she wanted more men to survive.

Critical Thinking answers will vary. Sample: People went to see Florence Nightingale instead of a doctor because she had so much experience with patients.

Summarize, p. 118

1. Hawaiian quilts are unique.
2. These quilts are made with the snowflake method.
3. Hawaiian quilts show the natural beauty of Hawaii.
4. Answers will vary. Sample: A Hawaiian quilt is easy to recognize because it has a natural design that is stitched to the background with white thread.

Critical Thinking answers will vary. Sample: Summary sentences help me to understand a text because they make it clear what each paragraph is about.

Summarize, p. 120

1. Answers will vary. Samples: Paragraph 1: Chesapeake Bay is a large bay surrounded by Maryland, Virginia, and the Atlantic Ocean, and many people visit it each year; Paragraph 2: Chesapeake Bay has some of the most famous coastal wetlands in the world; Paragraph 3: Chesapeake Bay has both freshwater and tidal wetlands; Paragraph 4: The freshwater wetlands of the Chesapeake Bay are just a few feet deep, while the tidal wetlands can be shallow or deep; Paragraph 5: Wetlands provide a home for plants that are able to live in water and wet soil all the time.
2. Answers will vary. Sample: The Chesapeake Bay is a large bay surrounded by Maryland, Virginia, and the Atlantic Ocean. This wetland provides habitats for both freshwater and tidal plants and animals.

Critical Thinking answers will vary. Sample: Summarizing the text helps me understand because I must decide what the overall main idea is.

Paraphrase, p. 122

1. Answers will vary. Sample: Long ago, families took care of each other; Families back then were not much different from families today; Long ago adults and children worked hard to get everything done; Adults today work hard, too, but most children do not have to work to keep the family going.
2. Answers will vary. Sample: Families back then and those of today are quite similar. The main differences are that today children no longer have to work and all the people in a family have more free time to spend together than in the past.

Critical Thinking answers will vary. Sample: My friend told me a funny story, and I had to paraphrase the story when I told it to another friend.

Paraphrase, p. 124

1. Answers will vary. Sample: The first clowns were called jesters, and they served in royal courts during the Middle Ages. In the early American circus, clowns were like comedians. Today, clowns perform at the circus and the rodeo. Each clown's costume and makeup are unique.
2. Answers will vary. Sample: Another word for *jester* is clown.
3. Answers will vary. Sample: A modern rodeo clown distracts dangerous animals so that hurt performers can escape.

Critical Thinking answers will vary. Sample: Summing up the text in my own words makes me think about what is important in the text and then decide how I want to say it.

Table of Contents, p. 126

1. The Digestive Tract
2. Answers will vary. Sample: I think that this chapter will be about why it is important to eat vegetables.
3. 9
4. I will read about the intestines.
5. page 18

Critical Thinking answers will vary. Sample: A book's table of contents is not in alphabetical order like the index. It is a listing of the chapters in the order in which they appear in the book.

Answer Key *(cont.)*

Table of Contents, p. 128

1. The Bison Bunch
2. Answers will vary. Sample: I predict that I will read about American Indians who lived in the desert.
3. 10
4. I will read about totem poles carvers.
5. page 4

Critical Thinking answers will vary. Sample: I would use a table of contents when I'm looking at library books to see the topics covered.

Index, p. 130

1. Answers will vary. Sample: The entries are listed alphabetically. I know because the page numbers are out of order but the words are listed in ABC order.
2. pages 15 and 19
3. I would read about arthropods and crustaceans.
4. page 14

Critical Thinking answers will vary. Sample: There is not an index in the back of a fiction book because it does not deal with facts that readers may need to look up.

Index, p. 132

1. Three other Clementes are mentioned in the book.
2. Answers will vary. Sample: Roberto Clemente is dead; He is in the Baseball Hall of Fame.
3. I will read about Roberto Clemente's childhood.
4. page 22

Critical Thinking answers will vary. Sample: A book's index is in alphabetical order but a table of contents lists things in the order in which they appear. Also, an index includes every concept discussed, even if only briefly, while a table of contents gives the "big picture" of chapter titles.

Glossary, p. 134

1. Answers will vary, but student must write two unfamiliar words listed in the glossary.
2. Student must write the definition of one of the words he or she listed in question 1.
3. Answers will vary. Sample: The blind man was able to read books in Braille.
4. Answers will vary. Sample: I sent my grandmother an email to ask how she was doing.

Critical Thinking answers will vary. Sample: I would use a glossary to look up the definition of a content word in a nonfiction text if I couldn't figure out its meaning using context clues.

Glossary, p. 136

1. Answers will vary, but student must write two unfamiliar words from the glossary.
2. Student must write the definition of one of the words he or she listed in question 1.
3. Answers will vary. Sample: They had to move to a new place because they were hungry due to the famine.
4. Answers will vary. Sample: This information in parentheses shows the pronunciation of the words.

Critical Thinking answers will vary. Sample: A glossary lists the meaning of words used in the book, but it doesn't tell the page where the word is used. The index lists these same words and tells on what page to find them, but it doesn't give the definition.

Contents of the Teacher Resource CD

Contents of the Teacher Resource CD (cont.)

Notes